It can truly be said that the life of Clara Louise Kieninger was one of selflessness and service. Yet more than that, her memoirs reveal a soul's initiation on the path that leads to reunion with God.

At the age of twelve, Clara Louise determined to be a nurse, and nothing would dissuade her from that calling. Upon graduation from Lutheran Hospital School of Nursing in St. Louis, she took her class motto, Ich Dien (I Serve) as the guiding principle of her life.

Wherever she served, Clara Louise left the mark of disciplined love even as she set the standard of perfection. Whether on the battlefield in World War I, in the founding of the first school of nursing in Brazil under the Rockefeller Foundation, or as director of nursing in schools and hospitals in the United States, she exemplified the true spirit of nursing—Ich Dien—in all that she did.

To follow the events of her life is to traverse with her the cycles of a service ever renewed as her soul, shuffling off this mortal coil, moved from the finite to the infinite expression of God's consciousness.

Ich Dien

The compelling memoirs of Clara Louise Kieninger, a woman whose life-style made her a true humanitarian.

Edited and compiled by Elizabeth Clare Prophet

SUMMIT UNIVERSITY 🔥 PRESS®
Corwin Springs, Montana

ICH DIEN
by Clara Louise Kieninger
Copyright © 1975, 2005 Summit Publications, Inc.
All rights reserved. First edition 1975
Second edition 2005

No part of this book may be reproduced, translated, or electronically stored, posted or transmitted, or used in any format or medium whatsoever without prior written permission, except by a reviewer who may quote brief passages in a review. For information, please contact:

Summit University Press
PO Box 5000
Gardiner, MT 59030-5000, USA
Tel: 1-800-245-5445 or 406-848-9500
Web site: www.summituniversitypress.com
E-mail: info@summituniversitypress.com

Library of Congress Control Number: 2005923321
ISBN: 1-932890-01-7

SUMMIT UNIVERSITY ♥ PRESS®

The Summit Lighthouse, *Pearls of Wisdom,* Science of the Spoken Word, Keepers of the Flame, Church Universal and Triumphant, and Summit University are trademarks registered in the U.S. Patent and Trademark Office and in other countries. All rights to their use are reserved.

Printed in the United States of America

Transferred to digital print on demand March 2005.

I dedicate this humble book to the great and glorious El Morya Khan, beloved Master, teacher, and friend, Chief of the Darjeeling Council, Darjeeling, India, who inspired the writing of it and who is tirelessly working with mankind, seeking to manifest in them the will of God on earth as it is in heaven.

CLK

Contents

A Word from the Editor   9
Preface to the Second Edition   14
A Word from Kuthumi   15
A Word from Mother Mary   16
A Word from the Great Divine Director   17

1   Growing Up   21
2   After Business College   27
3   Nursing   33
4   Graduation   45
5   War Service   57
6   At Home   65
7   Brazil   71
8   Denver   91
9   Wartime Service and Back to Brazil   101
10   New York   113
11   Service to the Masters   121
12   At the Summit of Life   131
13   The Promise of the Ascension   151
14   In the Twinkling of an Eye   155
    A Victory of Life   163
    The Annunciation of the Ascension   169
    The Central Temple of Ancient Lemuria   174
    Self-Discipline on the Path to the Ascension   179
    The Honor of God   186
15   Remembrances of Those Who Knew Her   189
    Notes   204
    Glossary   206

*Show me thy faith without thy works
and I will show thee my faith by my works.*
—James

A Word from the Editor

By the time the masters Morya and Saint Germain called me to serve at the Summit, Clara Louise Kieninger was already the Mother of the Flame. Upon the founding of the Keepers of the Flame Fraternity, Saint Germain had designated Clara Louise as one fully prepared in service, in discipline, and in love to keep the Flame of the Divine Mother on behalf of the sons and daughters of God on earth.

It was in 1961 that El Morya contacted me in Boston and said: "I have need of a feminine messenger. Go to Washington and I will train you through my messenger Mark Prophet." Ever since the age of eighteen, when I had seen the picture of Saint Germain, I had been waiting for the call to service under the spiritual hierarchy known as the Great White Brotherhood.* Thus when the call came, I was ready.

The first conference I attended was the Freedom Class held in Washington, D.C., over the July Fourth weekend in 1961. It was there that I met Louise. I looked through the congregation, seeing

---

* The Great White Brotherhood is a spiritual fraternity of ascended masters, archangels and other advanced spiritual beings. The term *white* refers not to race but to the aura of white light that surrounds these immortals. The Great White Brotherhood works with earnest seekers of every race, religion and walk of life to assist humanity. The Brotherhood also includes certain unascended disciples of the ascended masters.

for the first time a group of students who called themselves chelas of the ascended masters; they came from all over the United States and Canada, and there were may who were worthy of the name. But one stood out among them. Humble, soft-spoken, with a bearing of quiet dignity, she was there. And her presence was felt by all.

Clara Louise was not only a student of the masters. She was their friend. She knew them intimately. Through years of service in the field of nursing—a life lived in fulfillment of the Master's command "Inasmuch as ye have done it unto one of the least of these my brethren, ye have done it unto me"—Clara Louise served the body of God on earth, every part of that body, with the honor and the love which she would accord the Christ.

Her acquaintance with other members of the ascended hierarchy came in later years when she contacted representatives of the Great White Brotherhood and established her morning meditation for the world. From that time on, she called upon them daily as she kept the vigil of the Mother of the Flame, beginning her prayers at five in the morning and continuing from two to four hours on behalf of the youth of the world, the incoming children, their parents and teachers. She carried out this service every day of her life until God called her home.

Little did I know when I first laid eyes on her that she was not only a chela, but an initiate of the Great White Brotherhood —a chela who over the period of many incarnations had received the disciplines of a disciple and the initiations of a soul that aspired to the ultimate reunion with God, the ascension into the eternal Presence of the I AM THAT I AM.

In her final embodiment of service, Louise was continuing the walk with her Lord which she had begun as the Apostle James. It was a walk on the road to Emmaus that had never ended. It was the burning recollection of the experience on the Mount of Transfiguration. It was the fulfillment of the conviction of her soul that faith without works is dead. To her, Jesus was brother, master, and friend. How often I heard her admonish the young students of the masters as Mother Mary would have done. And when they would become involved in the trivial or in personality patterns, she would say, gently and yet with the authority of the Lord himself, "What is that to thee? Follow thou me!"

To those of us who were a part of the early years of the formation of The Summit Lighthouse and the masters' effort to contact their chelas throughout the world, Clara Louise was a light, an inspiration, and a tower of strength. When my training for the messengership was concluded under El Morya and Saint Germain anointed me as a messenger for the hierarchy, Louise was there. When the masters suggested that Mark and I be united for service in the ritual of marriage, Louise was there. And when our first child was born at Holytree House, Louise held him in her arms and gave him the blessing of the Mother of the Flame for a life of service to humanity.

As the years passed and Clara Louise was promised her ascension by Mother Mary, her friend the master El Morya requested that she write her memoirs so that sons and daughters of the Flame who would keep the Flame of Life for the children of God and carry the torch of illumination of the Divine Mother could follow in her footsteps. To read the story of her life is to participate in a meditation of discipline, one-pointedness, and constancy on a path of service that was preordained. Her sense of honor, her duty to her God, to her country, and to her fellowman took precedence over all else. In the East they call it dharma. It is one's duty to fulfill one's raison d'être. Dharma is the determination of the soul to conform to its true nature and to the principles of life as these move the soul from individual to cosmic levels of awareness.

In the path of service which Louise chose by her free will, she was fulfilling the mandates of karma yoga, that is, of actively balancing her karma through service to life. And her life as she reveals it in her memoirs is one of the perfect meshing of the dharma (duty) of the soul with its karma. It shows how the cause-effect sequences of the past (karma) are fulfilled in a way of life that becomes the soul's mission in the present. Through the path of service and the motto *Ich Dien* (I Serve), which she took upon graduation from the Lutheran Hospital School of Nursing in St. Louis, Missouri, Clara Louise attained, by the grace of God, her eternal freedom from the rounds of karma and the wheel of rebirth.

On October 25, 1970, the soul of Clara Louise took leave of the form which had served her well for eighty-seven years. At the time she was living with Mrs. Cecelia Lewis of Berkeley, California. It was during the birthday celebration of our third child that we received a call at the retreat in Colorado Springs from Mrs. Lewis that the transition had taken place. Our entire family and staff assembled in the chapel to commune with the soul of our precious mother at last born free. So great was her attainment that she ascended on the spot at the moment of her transition instead of being taken to the Retreat of the Ascension Flame at Luxor, Egypt, as is customary with candidates for the ascension.

The light from her Presence and the joy of her reunion with her beloved friends of light—with her teacher, Serapis Bey, with Mother Mary, whose presence she had become, and with her own twin flame, the ascended master Amen Bey—descended upon us like the gentle rain of the Holy Spirit. We meditated upon her life as the organ played her soul's keynote, "Calm As the Night," and Mark delivered the ascension service. On the third anniversary of her ascension, Clara Louise described her ascension experience and her service with the hosts of heaven in a dictation she gave through me to students of the ascended masters attending Summit University in Santa Barbara, California.

We have included this dictation, together with a subsequent dictation given November 10, 1974, as the fourteenth chapter of her memoirs.

As I prepared these pages for publication, I realized that the grand conclusion which we must draw from a life lived in God by one who walked among us is that by his grace we, too, can go and do likewise. By the example of our contemporary, one so near to our hearts, we are inspired to follow in her footsteps even as she followed in the footsteps of our Lord. Her victory gives us the hope that one day we, too, might leave behind the modes of time and space and enter the cycles of eternity.

As I read the memoirs of Clara Louise during the hours preceding the transition of my own Mark, I found myself merging with the spiral of her life. I traversed with her the cycles of a service ever renewed as her soul, shuffling off this mortal coil, moved from the finite to the infinite expression of God's consciousness. And it was in the simplicity of the words and the life of the first Mother of the Flame that I found the strength to bear the cross which all who would follow the Christ in the regeneration must bear. We therefore release these memoirs with the prayer that all who read them might find his strength and his unfailing love for a life of service and that all might espouse with the beloved Clara Louise the motto *Ich Dien*.

Elizabeth Clare Prophet
Mother of the Flame

Retreat of the Resurrection Spiral
Colorado Springs, Colorado
February 26, 1975

Preface to the Second Edition

The second edition of *Ich Dien* includes all the text and illustrations from the first edition of the book. It has been expanded to include the four dictations by Clara Louise given since the first edition was published.

On this, the thirtieth anniversary of the book's first release, we are very pleased to be able to make it available again after being out of print for some years. It is our hope that a new generation of lightbearers will now be able to draw inspiration from one whose dedication to service made a difference in so many lives.

The Editors
Summit University Press

A Word from Kuthumi

O sacred passion, Divine Love's reality, recognizing in all pure divinity, seeing no taint there nor effect of mortal soil, but only the royal figure of the Christ Child in all! This is to capture in time the form of eternal things to come.

A Word from Mother Mary

How tender is the flame of service! It is a living thing—invisible, yet visible in word and deed. It manifests the content of the jeweled casket of the heart; and it serves to tremble the harp of Life like unto angel hands that wipe away tears of human sorrow and, in the infinite, compassionate way of God, translate darkness and despair into Light.

The profession of nursing, when recognized as a divine opportunity, serves to bind up not only the physical wound, but also the inner hurts resulting from the clashes of life which infiltrate men's thoughts and feelings. Just as mankind seek to emulate the ladies of heaven, so the ladies of heaven seek to the present hour to reach out and express God's love through all serving hands and hearts on earth, through tongues attuned to heaven's pitch, through hearts inspired and inspiring.

If the magnificence of the Christ Child concept, leading individuals and nations to harmony and happiness, is to be realized, its meaning must be drawn closer to mankind by all who serve their many needs. The crowded marketplaces of life require love as much as does the mighty cathedral; and when the game is won and victory attained by the planet, it will be recorded as the deed of many hearts and many lives, not the least of which may be thine.

A Word from the Great Divine Director

The Golden Rule for all ages is "Do unto others as you would have them do unto you." This is the code which shall raise all civilization unto the permanent Golden Age. Fearless men and women are needed who can observe this rule in all their affairs. Now to *miss* the goal-target of understanding is *mis*understanding. No one, however, can *misachieve*. To do so is merely to be *mischievous*—and that without valiant purpose!

The unbounded energy of waste and disobedience always returns to the man or nation sending it forth. When virtue is enthroned in man and country as the ideal of each precious moment of life, the glorious civilizations that shall be born will lift up the garments of the world. No longer will civilization trail in the dust its garments of beauty and perfection. Wise rulers will exalt the divine tradition by noble acts daily performed.

South America, land of immortal promise! In thy domain is the future of mankind! Precious treasure of the Inca *(inner calling)!* The call of the Inca shall be revealed as truth in heart and mind behind the masks of confusing personality. The power of noble origin shall flash forth upon the screen of Reality to endure not for a moment, but as a shrine of the eternal kingdom to honor both Creator and created.

O goal-fittedness! O future purity! Appear now as the inspired moving of the coming race. Quicken the hearts of men and women today, and let the wind of the Holy Presence quiver both limb and trunk; let the unguents and the needed balm for healing be applied to the world, until the radiance of peace appears and men are spared needless pain.

What is that to thee? Follow thou me!
—Jesus

CHAPTER 1

Growing Up

Four generations ago my ancestors came from Saxony, Germany, and settled in Baltimore. Later they came to Missouri, where their descendants still live.

Mother was born in Missouri and at the age of nineteen was married there. She had several suitors, one the choice of her mother and the other her own choice. She was unhappy about her mother's choice. Mother's eighteenth birthday was celebrated with a party, and her mother promised that the first suitor to arrive (they had to come by horseback) would receive her consent to the marriage. Father had a much longer distance to come, but he arrived first. Grandmother, true to her word, made the announcement of the engagement. Mother and father were married, and the two elder children were born in Missouri.

Father brought his family to Kansas and they settled in Junction City. There was no church or religious school in Junction City, so the family decided to go to Topeka. By this time there were five children. I, the youngest, was four years old,* and the eldest was fifteen.

Before the family left Junction City, a pioneer friend, the mother of three sons, asked mother if she would look after her

---

* Clara Louise was born in Junction City, Kansas, on September 16, 1883.

boys should anything happen to her. Mother promised. Within two years, the mother of the boys passed on and the three brothers were brought to Topeka and became a part of our family. To our attic—large, roomy, and well-lighted—mother added three beds; and this served as a dormitory for five boys—my two brothers and the other three.

The three boys that came to us were Catholic. The eldest was sixteen, the youngest eleven. He was sent to the Catholic school to prepare for his confirmation. They were well trained, as all pioneer children were, and fitted well into our family life.

The eldest boy eventually found employment in a candy kitchen and later bought it. One of his chocolates is still on the market; it is one of the well-known delicacies. In a few years he returned to Junction City to the farm and married. The second boy found employment in a mill. The third one was interested in office work and found employment as an office boy. Later he became an executive in one of the large companies.

We lived on the corner, across the street from the church and school. My mother's sister lived in the middle of the block, next to the school, in a pretentious home. Our home was simple, but ample for all and happy.

The church was a stone structure. The ground floor served as the school, and the top floor served as the church. The pioneer families were closely knit. Many were families of affluence. All worked together to build Topeka, spiritually as well as socially and physically. Soon a schoolhouse was built and a teacher appointed. (Previously the minister had both the school and the church.) A parsonage was built next, and finally the new church.

When I was eight years old, a beautiful sister was born. We loved her dearly and she then and always has added to the joy of the family.

Mother was gracious, understanding, and patient. If she was ever discouraged or tired, we never knew it. She never complained, never once lost her courage and taught us never to lose ours, and when offense or disappointment came, to raise our souls so high that offense not could reach them. This helped through many trials. When we had small hurts or bruises, as children do, she would look at them, smile, and say, "That you will forget long before you get married."

Father was stern but kind, not always as patient and understanding as he might have been. His word was final. We saw the real father, though, when there was illness in the family. He grew kind and patient and in later years was fun. I once asked him why he had been so stern and so ready to punish. He answered, "To make you what you are today."

Our home was a gracious home. The door was never closed to anyone. All who needed help were always welcomed. Our playmates were always graciously received and always welcome to stay with us for meals. Mother was a wonderful church worker. We were trained by example and kindness what the Golden Rule really means and to practice it as she did.

In those days men started the day's work at 7:00 a.m., and in our home breakfast was served at 6:30. We children were up and ready for morning devotion by 6:15, fully dressed, combed, washed and happy. Mother and father were always the example. On winter nights after dinner there followed study hour, popcorn and apples, evening prayer, and bed. Mother heard our prayers at night. She had a sweet voice and taught us many lovely and sweet songs. Mother would sing with us until we fell asleep. I remember many of them and always have sung them and do now when sleep does not come quickly.

Father always asked the blessing at the table, and the youngest child followed with a sweet prayer. I was the youngest for eight years. We were taught early to thank God for every gift of life. How often mother would sing at her work. How often she would say, "I have my home, my children, and I am so grateful."

We never heard a complaint from her. We were taught to eat what was served, which was no hardship, for mother and the maid were excellent cooks. We were, as were all children, taught respect for elderly people. We did not curtsy, but always met and greeted elderly people graciously.

Mother and father were lovers of flowers and growing things. We had flower gardens. Father had a small vegetable garden. Many of the beautiful and fragrant flowers we had then are no more.

Everyone in the neighborhood had gardens; and at night after they were watered, the air was sweet with sweet fragrances and with sweet songs sung by mother and children. Sunsets were glorious. There were also bad storms—thunder and lightning. Mother taught us fearlessness. Thus the years sped on, a happy and joyous childhood.

I remember how thrilled I was at the confirmation services of my brother and sister. My uncle took my sister with him immediately thereafter to his home in the South, where she remained for five years, until mother thought she should come home and be part of the family again. I remember my reaction when I saw her. She had left, a lovely young girl; she now returned, a beautiful young woman of seventeen. She was married within a year to a young man who had fallen in love with a picture of her which she had sent to mother. He visited the family and saw the picture. After that there was no other girl for him. The families knew each other well and were delighted.

When he first came to see her after she returned home, he came only once a week, and ten o'clock was going-home time. Later he was allowed to stay until eleven. After about a year's courtship, which was fully supervised by my parents, they were married. This, of course, was not unusual; most families supervised their daughters' social life very carefully.

My sister and her husband had two beautiful daughters and

lived to celebrate their sixtieth wedding anniversary. They outlived both of their daughters. The elder daughter died in 1919 of encephalitis following influenza. The younger lived to be forty-seven years old, but was a semi-invalid all her adult life. Throughout the years, she was always a smiling, joyful example of fortitude to her many friends, who loved to visit her. No one left their home without feeling uplifted in spirit by her cheerfulness.

I was confirmed when I was twelve. Our preparation for confirmation was special classes in catechism and Bible study for two years before confirmation. These classes were held after school—twice a week the first year and three times a week the second year. We were orally examined, consecrated, and dedicated on Palm Sunday in the presence of the congregation. On Easter Sunday we had our first Communion. I took the confirmation and Communion very seriously; I trembled as I accepted beloved Jesus as my guide, and he has remained so all throughout these years.

Six years later I was graduated from Topeka Business College and received my diploma in business administration.

As children we were taught to be just and honest. The Golden Rule was so imprinted on us that we never forgot it.

One day mother received a small basket of lovely pears. One of them seemed to have disappeared. She asked who had taken it. No one answered. For some reason, she felt I had and asked me if I had taken it. I answered, "No, mother, I have not even touched them." She did not believe me. My punishment was—no pear. They were a rare delicacy and were enjoyed by the others. I did not care about the pear, but I did care that mother doubted me; and to this day I cannot eat a pear. In me was born that day the sense of justice, and the Goddess of Justice has been in my heart ever since.

On another occasion, when I was in the eighth grade, the

teacher accused me of cheating. Once a week we had a spelling test. We wrote the examination in a book which was kept by the teacher and passed out for the tests. There were no single desks. My seatmate, a brilliant student, was absent from the foregoing test and asked me if I would repeat the words of that test, which I did. Neither she nor I thought anything about it. Suddenly I heard the teacher say, "Louise, take the front seat." I took it, and the test continued. The test was always given fifteen minutes before noon. I remained behind when the class was dismissed and asked permission to speak to the teacher and said to her, "Since you accused me of cheating before the class, would you be kind enough to explain to the class that I was not cheating?" She answered that she would and said to me, "After you sat down, I realized my mistake." When the class assembled, she did apologize, and I was very grateful. Spelling and mathematics were two of my Red-E subjects.

Chapter 2

After Business College

My first position after graduating from business college was that of secretary to a rather small firm. Within a year, through a family friend in Los Angeles, I received a letter offering me a position as secretary to the managers of a new and beautiful winter resort hotel in Los Angeles. I was also to assist in the office. Because of the friendship, mother permitted me to go.

Among the guests of the hotel were a German baron and baroness. They were world travelers and spent much time in California, especially winters. There were four grown sons, the youngest finishing his senior year at Stanford University. The other sons were in business and had been in Los Angeles for several years. They did not live with their parents, but dined every night with them and always attended operas, concerts, and social affairs with them. Mr. and Mrs. Werner (they dropped their titles in the States) spent much time in the United States and made their temporary home at this winter resort hotel. Summers were usually spent in travel in Europe.

On one occasion it was necessary that Mr. Werner be absent from the city for a few days; and he asked at the desk, would we assist Mrs. Werner should she need help? Shortly after he left, a gentleman came to see him and, on finding him absent, asked to see Mrs. Werner. In a few minutes she came to the desk. She

looked distressed, so I asked her in German if I could help her. She was so relieved and grateful and, through interpretation, was able to take care of the business for which the gentleman had come.

Mr. Werner returned in a few days and called me to their suite. After asking permission from my chief, I went to see them. It was to thank me for that simple service I had rendered her and to offer me the position of social secretary to Mrs. Werner. Her secretary had resigned to be married. I replied that I would think it over, and consulted my chief. He said it would be a most interesting opportunity and experience and released me from my position with the hotel. I accepted the new position.

My duties were simple. We traveled a great deal. The first request he made of me was to get some timetables and plan a trip. In a few days we left on a trip to Arizona to look over some mining property in which he was interested and to attend a meeting with the syndicate. He asked me to attend that meeting, and I did. The meeting lasted several hours, and a glowing picture of the mine was presented to him. Mr. Werner did not commit himself but said he would let them know in a few days.

I offered no suggestions, but that evening he asked my opinion. I replied: "I would never trust that syndicate out of my sight—or even in it! I would not invest one penny in that scheme." Arizona and the West were full of swindlers, and I would trust none of them. There were honest ways of investing money. Mr. Werner did not invest and we left the next day for Los Angeles. Arizona was not then what it is today, but I loved it. The hotel in which we stayed was a simple building, two stories high, one bathroom on each floor, no conveniences of any kind. The state was beautiful.

The Werner sons, who lived in a downtown hotel, had dinner with us every evening and also accompanied us wherever we went—to concerts, theaters, operas, etc. I remember the first night at dinner. Our table was in the center front of the dining room. It was a time of formal dinner dress. Mrs. Werner sat at Mr. Werner's right, I at his left, the sons around the table. A toast was proposed to me. I put the glass to my lips but did not drink. When Mr. Werner noticed that I did not drink the wine, he asked the reason.

I replied, "I do not drink wine, Mr. Werner."

He insisted that I do—gave me reasons why I should.

Finally I said: "Mr. Werner, if you persist, I will leave the table. Not now or any other time will I drink wine or any other alcoholic beverage." I never have.

Mr. Werner decided we must go to the seashore, to Long Beach. The town then had one hotel two stories high, a few shops, some cottages, and a few homes. (Imagine then and now!) The sea was calm and beautiful: it was heavenly. The sons were to come for weekends.

We came to breakfast the following morning to great excitement. There had been an earthquake in San Francisco* and the city was in flames. It was declared out of bounds, as was Oakland. Mr. Werner wanted to see the damage in San Francisco. As soon as Oakland was open, we journeyed there and waited another week before San Francisco was accessible. Then Mr. Werner hired a phaeton and we went over. I had been in San

---

* April 18, 1906.

Francisco before, when it was a thriving city. Now, from where we were, nothing but bare hills could be seen. Not a tree, not a house was left standing. We returned to Oakland and remained there for another week, during which time slight shocks could be felt every day. Then we returned to Los Angeles.

In the meantime, one of the sons became engaged to a lovely heiress, and a fashionable wedding was planned. At that time weddings were held at high noon. Mr. Werner decided that Mrs. Werner should have a hat to wear at the wedding—a stylish American hat. She always wore beautifully tailored suits and wore the bonnet-type hat tied under her chin with a bow, a real German *mütterchen*.

Off we were, Mrs. Werner and I, to the finest stores to try on hats. Mr. Werner did not go with us. She tried on hats and hats with never a word of complaint; like a lamb she submitted to what must have been great discomfort. I felt sorry for her and declared, "Enough of that torture." With the help of clerks, we selected a modest but good-looking hat and returned to the hotel. There really was not a hat suitable for her.

Mr. Werner was waiting expectantly. When he tried the hat on her and saw what she looked like in it, he made a few heartfelt remarks and said he was going to buy her a hat, the kind of a hat he visualized, and he was going alone. Off he went downtown himself to buy a hat. When he returned to the hotel and showed it to us, she said not one word nor did I. It was a beautiful creation, a light-colored straw hat with pink roses and lovely blue-velvet ribbon, really suited for a young woman. He tried this hat on her and saw how she looked in it; he was furious, said not one word, and tore the hat to pieces. He was trying to make of her a stylish American woman. Hats were never mentioned again.

For the wedding Mrs. Werner was dressed in a beautiful suit, but she did wear her bonnet. They presented me with a model dress and a model hat; they were simple and very beautiful.

After Business College

I wondered how the marriage would work out; but it did work out and they were very devoted and happy and had a family of several children.

The members of the family were devoted to each other. We had a happy life and months passed very quickly. The sons accepted me as one of them. But I knew it could not go on, as I was interested in more serious matters.

One evening Mr. Werner called me to their suite and told me about a contemplated trip to Egypt. Their only daughter had died in Egypt and was buried there, and they often made pilgrimages to her grave. I knew that was the end of my stay with them, as mother would never consent to my going out of the country with them. When Mrs. Werner excused herself and left the room, I got up also. Mr. Werner said he had something to talk over with me: would I please stay. He opened the subject with the question "Do you like Bernhardt?"

I replied: "Yes, I do. I like all of your sons. We've had so much fun together and they've been so wonderful."

"I know that, but particularly, do you like Bernhardt? He is in love with you. We love you too. He wishes to marry you, and we wish it too."

"But I don't love Bernhardt. I don't want to marry him or anyone."

"What's love got to do with it?"

He talked with me at length about it and then said, "The day you marry Bernhardt, we will settle a dowry of $50,000 upon you."

I said: "But I don't want to marry him, Mr. Werner. There is not enough money in this world to buy me."

Before I left the suite that evening, he said, "I want to show you something" and took out his wallet. From it he took his daughter's picture and a lock of her hair, and beside it was a lock of my own. He said: "This is how we love you. You have been like a daughter to us and we would like you to stay with us." I do not know how he got a lock of my hair.

I knew then that I would have to leave them. Mother had been asking me to come home. I told him I would leave in a few days; and he replied that they would be going then too, but they would stop in my home on their way back from Europe and pick me up. He would write or telegraph the train number, the day, and the time so I would be at the station ready to come back with them. I told him I would be happy to see them and would like my parents to meet them, but it would be useless because mother had said no, I must stay home.

I was disappointed in a way, and yet I knew that even if mother had said yes, I would not go. I had other plans. It was not the kind of life I wanted. Later, father said that he was sorry mother took the stand she did, for they could not give me the advantages that the Werners could; but I said, "Never mind, father, I have other plans."

We parted, the Werners and I. It was a sad parting in a way. We had been together and had fun; we swam together, played together, traveled together, and were always together in the evenings. Then I left.

Mother, of course, was glad to have me come home; and when I told her they wanted me to return, she said *no* with an emphasis that told me she meant it. She forbade me to write to them. I did have a letter from them; and when they returned, I met them at the station for a few minutes while the train stopped. Mother would not go to meet them. I told them how mother felt, and I respected her wishes and never saw them again. If they wrote to me, I never received the letters—mother saw to that. I felt there was a reason for this turn of events, for I wanted to fulfill my divine plan and felt this was not it.

CHAPTER 3

Nursing

As a child I had never cared for or played with dolls. There were a number of children in our neighborhood and we played happily and joyously together. My sister was the dressmaker for all the dolls in the neighborhood. For Christmas one year I had received a laundry set consisting of a little bench, a washboard, tub, wringer, two buckets, clothespins, and wash lines. How I loved it! I washed all the doll clothes in the neighborhood and then washed everything else in sight.

We also loved dressing up and making mud hats. We had a picket fence around our home, which was on the corner, and often the fence was full of mud hats. Of course, I had to clean them up.

When I was about twelve, mother took me with her to the hospital one afternoon to visit a very close friend of the family. When the graduate nurse came into the room in her immaculate white uniform, that was my answer. I knew then what it was that I wanted to be. I talked to mother about it many times, but she was adamant in her refusal. No daughter of hers was going to be a nurse and take care of men lying in bed. This was not an unusual attitude for that generation. However, I was determined, and on my return from California I wrote to various hospitals for catalogs. Our good friend the family physician was my inspiration.

I had been getting catalogs and other material together for months when mother realized what I was doing and again was adamant. In the meantime, I had been offered a position with a large department store and accepted it. In a short time I was made head of the department, and later, buyer. However, I never relinquished for a moment my determination to be a nurse. I was two years convincing my mother that nursing was my goal and I would never give up.

Those two years at home were happy years, gracious and full of fun. I never regretted that I had them with my family and friends. It was the last time I was really ever at home for any length of time. Our home was a home for young people. Father was an excellent cardplayer, and often he and the boys played cards. With so many young people around, he became fun.

Our yard was a large one with croquet, swings and seesaws, horseshoes, etc. On Sundays the yard was usually filled with young people. Many of these were girls from farms and small towns who came to Topeka to work in order to earn enough money to go to school or build hope chests and later marry. Mother always prepared the buffet dinner on Saturday to be served on Sunday and invited all who were away from their own home to come and share it with us. We girls were not always at home, but there were always boys on hand—my brother and his friends.

We owned two horses, and when I was a child, father often put me on one and led me around our large yard. My love for horses began then. I rode a great deal in later years and learned to ride in a divided skirt. (The sidesaddle was losing its popularity.) My mother was an excellent rider; most pioneers were, as it was their way of getting around.

One Sunday, shortly after I arrived home, one of my friends, a great lover of horses who owned several thoroughbreds, asked me to take a canter with him. I was delighted. I had been trained the Western way of riding, and as I turned the horse, I forgot and turned him by the neck instead of the bit. The horse reared (I was on an English saddle), stood on his hind feet, and I slid off his back and onto the streetcar track and injured my back. The horse waited. I got up and we rode on, but not too far. I got over that, and that afternoon I poured at a tea in pain. However, later I really felt the effects of that fall, and mother forbade my riding again.

When mother saw how determined I was to become a nurse, she at last consented but felt she should talk it over with one of our family friends. Between them, they decided that if I entered a church hospital for training, I might go. I was admitted in the fall class and with joy departed for the Lutheran Hospital Nursing School in St. Louis, Missouri.

Finally I arrived in St. Louis with a joyful and hopeful heart to report to the director of the school of nursing. The National Nurses Association had changed by law the nursing curriculum from a two-year to a three-year course. Our class was the first to enter under the new three-year regulation and was not large.

The director—a tall, dignified woman in immaculate white—greeted me graciously. Her assistant then escorted me to my room in the nurses' dormitory. She announced that supper would be served at five o'clock and someone would come to accompany me to the dining room.

The room to which I was assigned was small. It was large enough to hold two small beds with a small chest of drawers between. In the corner was a small closet for our clothes and a very small table and one chair. All the dormitory rooms opened into the central hall, or room, and this in turn opened on a large terrace.

I think I had idealized nursing and everything with it and admit I was disappointed by the setup. But in a few minutes my roommate appeared to take me to supper. She was tall and beautiful and in introducing herself said: "I know how you feel. I felt the same way." Then I remembered what mother had said: Hold your head high, square your shoulders, put on a bright smile, and carry on. That ended my feeling of disappointment, and I was really ashamed that I had not been a better sport.

Since our class was not large, we members became close friends and have remained so. I remember that as I entered the dining room and saw the graduate nurses in their immaculate white and the student nurses in their blue, my heart thrilled anew with the thought of becoming one of them. I knew I would never give up and never have.

Our first formal meeting the following morning was our orientation class with the director. She explained the reason for rules, obedience, and discipline and that we would be on probation for six months. She said that life is the most precious and greatest gift in the universe and that to take care of that life is the greatest service anyone can render, that obedience was imperative.

We were indoctrinated in the strict military discipline: we were never to step in front of a graduate nurse, never to step in front of a senior or a junior nurse. We were probationers in the true sense of the word. We were to do as we were told, not to argue, never to question unless we did not understand. We were not to address a senior or junior nurse unless we were spoken to, and certainly not to go out with them socially. Nor were we to go out alone with young men, but must always go out in threes. We were to stand in the presence of the supervisors, doctors, the staff, and the uniformed nurses, not to carry on conversation on the wards unless it was professional—even a junior dared not speak to the director on duty unless it was professional. We were assigned our first duties. Mine was to clean the bathrooms and keep them clean in the nurses' dormitory.

The next morning after breakfast, I stepped into the bathroom. When I saw the condition of it, I decided I would not clean it and reported to the ward to which I had been assigned (the women's surgical ward). I felt I would be called to the director's office. In about an hour the head nurse of the ward asked me to report to the director in the dormitory. I reported. Stately in her dignity, she asked me if I were in charge of the bathrooms. I replied, "Yes, Miss G——."

She said, "Come with me" and led me to the bathroom. I knew, of course, that it did not pass her inspection. They were just as the nurses had left them that morning. She asked me if I called that clean and orderly.

I replied, "No, Miss G——."
"Will you clean it now?"
"No, Miss G——."
"You refuse?"
"Yes, Miss G——."

I said: "I am willing to do what is right, but I did not enter this school of nursing to clean the bathrooms after nurses, especially the junior and senior students who are soon to graduate. By now they should have learned how to wait upon themselves and not expect others to wait upon them. I came to learn the art and care of the sick and not to wait upon nursing students."

She asked, "Is that your answer?"
"Yes, Miss G——."

I was not sure if she would send me home for insubordination; but the situation was taken care of without another word, in fairness and justice. The probationers were relieved from waiting on students.

My first ward assignment was on the women's ward, two- and three-bed wards. We learned to give baths, make beds, take care of bedside tables, and general sanitation of the wards and bathrooms. We received our practical experience on the wards at the bedside of the patient under supervision, and it was thorough. Duty hours were from 7:00 a.m. to 7:00 p.m., twelve hours, with two hours a day off *if* we could get them and one half-day a week. Sometimes class came on an off-duty hour and on the half-day. Night duty was three months, twelve hours, without a day off. Classes came out of our sleeping time, and we had one day off at the end of our night-duty term. It was really our "night" sleeping day before assignment to another service. We were given two weeks' vacation in the summer. We affiliated three months each for pediatrics and obstetrics, as there was no maternity or pediatric department in any hospital at that time. My operating-room service was six months instead of three, and it was thorough.

After one month's service, I was made charge nurse under the surgical supervisor and was responsible for the perfect service, cleanliness, and sterilization of the rooms, the gloves, and the instruments. The operating supplies had to be made; instruments had to be cleaned, kept separate, and put into the doctors' instrument cases. The gloves had to be mended and sterilized, and surgical supplies packed and sterilized. The operating-room floor had to be scrubbed on our knees until it was as gleaming white as the white uniforms before we left at night, no matter how late. We were always on call for emergency operations at night.

There were three students besides myself working in perfect harmony. We were young and strong. It was all a challenge. We had a good friend, the cook, who often after a busy morning or afternoon sent us a pot of fresh coffee and fresh-baked coffeecake and rolls. The six months passed very quickly. We had very few hours off (except for classes) and usually worked late into the evening, but we learned a great deal. It was a wonderful experience in training and discipline. I enjoyed the service, but I knew I would never choose it. Before my operating-room service

I was in charge of the emergency and dressing room.

After I finished the operating-room service, I was asked to report to the director's office. She asked if I had ever had scarlet fever. I answered yes. Diphtheria? Yes. Typhoid fever? Yes. Also one or two other children's diseases. I answered, "Yes, Miss G——" to everything she asked me. She said: "There has been an outbreak of scarlet fever in the orphans' home, and there are four very ill patients and others coming down with it. Be ready by six o'clock and you will be taken there." I was thrilled.

We arrived at 10:00 p.m. The housemother and father greeted us. The graduate nurse was ready to go back with the automobile that brought me. She did not wait long enough to give me a report of the sick. I remember how shocked I was that a graduate nurse would not even stay long enough to give a report to the succeeding nurse because it was charity. However, I put on my uniform and started my work. (We never wore our uniforms on the streets or off duty.)

There were thirty children in the two wards. I stayed up all night. Four of them were very ill, and there were several suspects. It was necessary to separate them from the other children and move them from the home. Within a stone's throw was the old orphans' home in excellent condition, beautifully situated on a small lake in a grove of beautiful trees. It lent itself very well to our purpose. There were several very large rooms and a very large hall between on the first floor. The same on the second floor. The next morning we equipped it and moved six patients into it. In a few days more were admitted. We had in all twenty patients. There was one very ill diphtheria patient who needed constant care and passed on in a few days. The doctor was retired and came often. The mother and father of the home came to the porch several times a day, always in the morning and at night.

They sent an elderly patient to help me. Prepared meals were sent from the home. I walked to the lake every evening when

I could. Sunsets were a great benediction. I was to be maid of honor at the wedding of my favorite cousin in early October. I had planned my vacation around it. It looked as if I would be able to go if there were no more sick children. The assistant could take care of the convalescents. The children were well trained and easy to care for.

We had a potbelly-stove heater. It was cool in the evenings, and I always lighted it in the early evening, admonishing the children not to touch it and the assistant to watch. I kept the door open so the children could watch the glow. I never stayed at the lake longer than fifteen minutes, sometimes only five to ten minutes. One evening when I returned, a chorus of voices greeted me: "Oh, Nurse, Bob played with the fire!"

I always left the stove door open for the children to enjoy the glow. I took the child by his hand, protected by my own, and held them to the glowing fire. He became frightened. I took him on my lap and explained to him and the other children the danger of it—the pain of the fire if it burned them and how quickly it spread. I asked them if they understood; if not, to ask whatever they wanted to know about fire and I would tell them. Never again was there any problem with fire. I always listened to their prayers in the evening. We would often sing. It was sweet. They were dear children.

Time was speeding on. The first of October was approaching. The doctor said I could go. There seemed to be no more suspects. I prepared everything to make it easy for my assistant—shampooed my hair, etc. In the morning I was to leave for St. Louis, then on to Topeka for the wedding. The next morning the father and mother came down as usual (I thought) to see if I were ready. When I saw tears in the mother's eyes, I knew what that meant. Another patient ready to come down. The doctor feared there would be more.

I smiled and said, "Remember, mother, I am a nurse; and

that is a part of nursing." I asked her if they would telegraph my family that I would not come home for the wedding, to give my beautiful maid-of-honor dress to the young woman who would take my place as maid of honor. I put on my uniform and carried on. In a week would be the wedding. If there were no more patients within two weeks, I would be able to leave. I went to the lake more often and felt the peace of that beautiful small lake and the glorious sunsets.

Fortunately, the child was not very ill; and if there were no more suspects, I would be able to leave at the end of the two weeks, leaving the care of convalescent patients to my assistant. There were no more patients.

I did not go home. The wedding was over. I spent the two weeks with a favorite cousin and her precious family in a small town and a cousin who came from the South to visit us.

On my return to the hospital, I was placed in a private pavilion as the head nurse. In the morning report, the night nurse reported a new patient had come in late at night for observation. He would not let the nurses do anything for him. He was an old bachelor and very unpleasant, she said.

In my rounds after the report, I knocked gently on this patient's door and opened it. He greeted me with "What do you want in here? Get out! I've never been bossed by a woman and I don't intend to start now."

I replied, "I came in to ask if you have a special wish for breakfast."

He replied: "You should know what a patient needs. Send it in, and do not come back." I sent it in to him.

Presently the bell rang and he asked that I come in. He was sitting up in bed with his breakfast tray on his lap. He said, "What do you call this? What kind of breakfast is this?"

I took the tray out and sent in another one. He said, "Now get out."

Before I left his room, I asked him to remove his silk union suit. He answered: "I will do no such thing. I am not going to be bossed by a woman."

I answered, "How can the doctor give you a thorough examination with it on?"

He replied: "That is none of your business. Now get out and stay out."

I did accompany the doctor on his rounds. He said to the doctor: "Send that woman out. I never had a woman waiting on me and I don't intend to begin now." I left the room. However, there were certain things that women had to do for him. In time he became softened and became a good patient. (We graduated in the fall of the year, and I invited him to the graduation.)

He called me into his room one day. He was sitting up in bed, and on his lap was a large tray of beautiful jewels. He said: "I want you to select whatever jewel or jewels you wish. They were my mother's, and I wish you to have some of them." I looked the tray over and selected a very simple gold bar pin. He said, "I want you to take another pin, one of these diamond ones." I did not take any that he indicated, but finally selected an ivory rose and chain, which I wore later to all the early morning classes of Mother Mary. He insisted that I select some gorgeous piece, but to no avail. In a few days he was dismissed from the hospital; and for my graduation he sent two dozen gorgeous American Beauty roses, a five-pound box of candy, and twenty-five dollars. Also, he came to the graduation, but left immediately after the service. I never saw him after that.

A soft answer turneth away wrath. In this particular patient, it brought about a complete change from a sour, bitter person to an understanding and friendly being.

The three years of training had been busy and full of hard work, but also full of opportunities, experiences, and accomplishments. The sweet smile on a sick child's face, the shining love and light in the eyes of a new mother, the beauty of a newborn child, the gratitude over the recovery of a member of a family; a flower, a shiny apple, a few pieces of homemade candy, or a tiny gift brought in by some lonely and poor patient who had been helped; the respecting gratitude of the medical profession—all these were jewels that paved a path into the entrance of a life of service.

CHAPTER 4

Graduation

We thrilled at the consecration and dedication when we received our caps. In a few days we were to be rededicated and reconsecrated. We took our graduation seriously. A week before the baccalaureate service, one of our classmates contracted diphtheria and passed on in four days. Another one had a mild case of it. We were not permitted inside the church for the baccalaureate service. Our classmate was to be buried that day—Sunday. We were permitted to attend the burial. We were *not* permitted to get out of the limousine.

On the following Sunday evening we wore our white graduating uniform and caps and received our diplomas in a beautiful and consecrated service in the church. I realized then why mother had insisted on my entrance to a church hospital, and my gratitude to her is deep. On Wednesday evening there was chapel for patients and for all who wished to attend. Patients enjoyed the singing and organ music and the service.

With the long path before me, I seemed to look into eternity. There would be many doors open on that path, and my entrance into and through them would be *Ich Dien* [I Serve]—chosen as our class motto—guided by the Father, the beloved Master Jesus, and my own beloved Guru, my Teacher.

Just before graduation, I was called into the director's office and offered the position of assistant floor supervisor. Although I felt I needed much further training, I accepted and began my duties immediately.

In a short time mother wrote that she needed surgery and asked if I would come home and take care of her. I asked her to come to St. Louis to our hospital. She came. In those days laboratory tests were not made as a routine. She was taken into the operating room. The operation was found to be a very, very minor thing, and seemingly she made an uneventful recovery and was taken home. However, she had had ether. In about two weeks my family called me to come home, that mother had had a convulsion.

I knew what that meant. Laboratory tests showed a deep involvement of kidneys. Mother had developed a serious kidney condition. I found her irrational and semiconscious. I took care of her for six months, having moved her bed to the back parlor, as we called it then, and never in the six months left home nor her bedside. She was desperately ill. On several occasions the doctors said she could not possibly live through the night. I placed my morris chair beside her bed and at night tied her big toe to my little finger so the slightest movement would awaken me had I fallen asleep, and that was my bed for almost six months.

One day father said to me: "I think it time for you to get some rest. I will watch mother tonight." I said, "I will lie on the couch in the room to be on call." I heard an awful bump. I knew what it meant. Mother had fallen out of bed. Father was terribly distressed. I remember I sent a prayer and asked God to care of him and give him peace. Mother, unconscious, was on the floor, a dead weight. The bed was high. I don't know how I ever got her into bed by myself. Father was walking the floor in the kitchen. I put her in a warm pack. I did not tell my sister, who slept upstairs, but I never left her bedside again while she was a bed patient.

She had had a slight stroke and it had affected her eyes. After she was convalescent, our physicians arranged with the optician to bring down his apparatus and examine her eyes. I had not asked for it. Although they knew there was nothing to be done, he did it to please her. I was told she could live only two years; but with wonderful care from my sister, she lived a happy and serene life for eight years.

During her illness father contracted pneumonia. Fortunately he was not too ill. I had two patients for a while. I learned much about home care for the sick. I cannot *ever* forget the kindness of members of the medical profession. It was never too late for them to call, by phone or person, never too early in the morning or late at night to come. They came often and telephoned several times a day. They were a tremendous comfort.

When mother was convalescent, I decided to go back to St. Louis. Since I knew even before I entered nursing school that my goal was some day to be a director of nursing, I wished to prepare myself to teach and guide nursing students from firsthand information. In order that I might go back to St. Louis and follow my chosen profession, my sister gave up a very responsible position. Mother needed someone with her, although she needed no real care. I brought the medical bills with me. The care I gave mother and the paying of the expenses in connection with her illness, I felt, would in some little way repay her for what she had done for the family.

Two years ago I was in Topeka in a flower market to buy some flowers, and in came one of the doctors, the youngest of the several who took care of mother. I could not speak. His kindness, his courtesies, his selfless service rushed before me, and my eyes filled with tears. He put his arms around my shoulders, then walked out without a word. He recently passed on.

I returned to St. Louis and was invited to stay at the exclusive Graduate Nurses Club, for which I was deeply grateful. The club was well known, and the calls were many, personal and otherwise. I knew the kinds of homes and patients I wanted for the experience, and they seemed to come, one after another. Surely I was led and guided. It was as if someone had selected them for me, and I accepted that they had been.

My first patient was a heart case, twelve-hour night duty in a small, three-room home. They were foreigners. The family consisted of mother, father, a little girl of about three, and a baby of six months. The mother was the patient. The father worked in a packing house at night.

I arrived about eight o'clock in the evening. It was July, summertime. The house was like an oven. The mother was wet with perspiration. The children were crying. I changed into my uniform, took the mother's pulse, straightened her bed, washed her face and hands, and rubbed her back. I then asked her if it were agreeable to her for me to take care of the children before I finished her. She was grateful for this. After I had finished bathing, feeding, and putting them to bed, it was nearly midnight. I then started with the patient. Before I finished with her, she had fallen asleep. Her long hair was a mass of tangles. I did not touch it that night. I was grateful that she was sleeping. The children were sleeping.

Then I went into the kitchen. Fortunately I had brought an apron with me. I can never forget that kitchen! The table was stacked with dirty dishes and the sink full of cooking utensils. Even the floor was cluttered with pots and pans. I rolled up my sleeves and set to work, washed the dishes, swept the floor, set the table for the father's breakfast, fixed the coffee ready to boil, and set the pan out for the eggs and the bacon.

Back into the sickroom to give the mother her bath preparatory for the day, to dress the little girl, to take care of the baby, and to feed the children. When I suggested that I would like to comb her hair, the patient exclaimed: "Oh, no! You must not touch my hair. In my country we never touch anyone's hair when they are sick. It is bad luck." I do not remember what I said, but later she permitted me to brush her hair for the day and pin it up for her. Then she admitted that it really did feel better.

She made a rapid recovery and I was with them five nights. They were so grateful they asked me to go to church with the father on Sunday, as he wished to make a novena to Mother Mary in gratitude for his wife's recovery. I did not go with him.

Two or three weeks later I received a huge box. When I opened it, it was full of every kind of sausage one could imagine. It was their way of expressing their gratitude. I was deeply touched. The nurses were happy over the choice sausages. A note of appreciation for the sausages was the last contact I had with them.

I did not spend much time in the club, but was called from one patient to another. My second patient was in the hospital for surgery; but the patient was nonoperative and the family took him home, and me with them. This was one of the affluent families in St. Louis. It was twenty-four-hour duty, and my room was next to his. I was on call at night also. He needed very little nursing. When he needed intensive care, another nurse was called. Each of us was on twelve-hour duty, but the family would not let me leave the house at night. Even though the other nurse was on night duty, I still retained my room.

When he passed away, his family would not permit him to be taken to a mortuary for preparation for burial and had the mortician come to the house with all the apparatus to embalm him. They asked me to stay in the room until he was ready for the coffin, which I did. I finally returned to the club. They sent for me for the funeral. They asked me to stay with them and make my home with them, but I had other plans.

The third patient was a little girl of three years, a tracheotomy patient. She needed constant watching; she would pull the inner tube out of the large tube in her neck. However, she made a good recovery. In three weeks I accompanied her to her home. Her family consisted of the father, mother, and five children, the youngest six months and the oldest eight years. They lived on a beautiful plot of ground, well wooded, at the edge of the city, and owned a well-established tavern, served a good class of people. Their especially busy days were Saturday nights and Sundays.

There was not much to do for the patient. As the mother seemed very tired, I took over the care of the six-month-old baby and the children as well as my patient. We spent the days in the garden and in the woods. Since there was not very much to do, I asked the mother if there were any mending or darning she would like me to do. She was delighted and brought a large basket full of socks and stockings that needed darning and some mending. Darning socks for the family was one of my home chores when I was growing up, and father often complimented me on the fine job I did. (A compliment from father meant a great deal to us.)

I also made the baby's feedings and took general care of him. Telling stories, keeping the older children busy, darning socks, and taking care of the baby kept me quite busy. But it was a service I gladly rendered to a tired and weary mother. At night I put the five children to bed. They were Catholic, and only mother could hear their prayers. No matter what she was doing, she always stopped and listened to their prayers.

After a week or ten days, I felt I was no longer professionally needed and asked the surgeon to terminate my services. The mother asked me if I would remain and make my home with them. She had been an only child and never had a sister or anyone close to her; and for the first time she knew what it must be like to have a sister, someone in the home who cared and understood. She asked me if I would just stay with them and help her with the children. However, I felt I must carry on with my chosen service.

In the early days it was not unusual to do operations in the homes, especially in smaller towns. One of the surgeons asked me to accompany him to do an operation on a young boy, sixteen years old. It seemed to be an emergency. His family would not consent to have him brought to the hospital.

The surgeon's father was the family physician. He would prepare the patient and set up the room and have all ready for our arrival. We arrived in the evening. The surgeon examined the patient and found the patient could wait until morning, and he decided to return to St. Louis. The local doctor gave the patient a sedative, and the patient fell asleep. I decided to get some sleep also. My bed was in the room next to the patient. It was an old-fashioned folding bed. When I opened it, it had no mattress, only a thin comforter on the spring. The linen was immaculate. I stood there a few moments, then decided to get what sleep I could. Was up a few times to see the patient; I found him sleeping. I slept also.

Up early the next morning for final preparation for the operation. Soon the surgeon arrived. I sterilized the instruments, gave the anesthetic. The father of the surgeon assisted with the operation. By nine o'clock the operation was over. There was no rupture. The patient, although quite ill, made an uneventful recovery.

There was no running water or bathroom in the home, and I looked around to find a place for bathing. The mother was quite heavy, had a heart condition, and carried two buckets of water from across the street every day. As soon as I could leave the patient, I offered to carry the water for her. She refused, but finally let me do it. I told her I needed the exercise. There was a cistern for rain water in the yard.

I took my meals with them. There was a white tablecloth on the table, only at my place. The other part of the table was covered with oilcloth. I suggested that we all eat on oilcloth, as it would be more friendly. She finally consented. I could not see that precious, worried mother washing white tablecloths and napkins at the time I was with them!

This was in May. They lived on the corner, had a lovely yard, beautiful trees, and a beautiful rose garden in bloom. It was a village of roses. The rose fragrance permeated the atmosphere of the little village. I was looking for a place to bathe and finally decided that between the beautiful rose bushes I could take baths at night, when the little village was asleep, and be safe from onlookers!

When the boy was fully recovered and I was ready to leave, the mother asked me what she could do for me to show her gratitude. Also the neighbors wanted to know what they could do for me. The little village wanted to buy a gift to show their gratitude and appreciation. They had been apprehensive at the thought of a graduate nurse coming into their midst, but had soon learned that there was nothing to fear. I could not refuse to accept this offer of friendship and told her the dearest gift they could give me was to gather rose petals for a rose-petal pillow. When I was ready to go, they brought a huge pillow slip full of rose petals. This deeply touched my heart. Even now as I write, the tenderness of it fills my heart and the fragrance of those rose petals is with me.

I had been with them two weeks, and now the mother could take care of the boy herself. It was a delightful experience. I was friendly with the neighbors, and all of them came to see us when we returned to St. Louis.

My fifth and last patient was the son of a famous internist. He had contracted typhoid fever, but it was a mild case and he was not very ill. He was a delightful child of about ten years, and we spent much time reading and playing games. I was with them ten days even though the child did not really need me.

The boy loved chewing gum and swallowed some. He became very frightened, as did his mother. I assured her it would not hurt him; but being a mother, she called the doctor unbeknown to me. He assured her it would not hurt him. She told her husband what she had done. He told her she should not have called the doctor. The nurse knew. What she told you was true. She told me what she had done and apologized. "No apology needed. You are a mother. Were I one, I would probably have done the same thing." I was with them ten days. A most delightful family. The boy gave me his most-loved book; the doctor gave me a valuable medical book.

I felt that the experience that I had had in the field of private duty would be invaluable, and I found that it was.

At this time I received an offer of position as assistant director of a school of nursing and of a 200-bed hospital in a nearby city, which I accepted with great anticipation.

In my school days there were no obstetrical or children's department in hospitals, and students received their experience through affiliation in those special hospitals. Obstetrical patients were rarely admitted in general hospitals. However, an exception was made for the chief obstetrician and gynecologist in this hospital, whose special patient and friend was coming from Texas to be delivered by him. After morning report I visited the preoperative patients, the postoperative patients, and the very ill patients. I visited this patient's room; and when I opened the door, she cried, "Oh, Miss K., come in, come in! I think I am delivering my baby!" There was no time to ring for the intern, no time to set up a table or ring for a nurse.

I stepped to the bed, and in a few minutes the baby was delivered. I remember making a prayer that there would be no tears, no hemorrhage, no complications, and that it would be a clean delivery. Also that the obstetrician or one of the interns would come. There was no time even to undo a sterile package. I was just about ready to tie the cord when the door opened, and there stood the chief obstetrician, the man for whose service she had traveled a thousand miles! I asked him to *please* tie the cord.

He stepped to the bed and said: "You tie the cord. You're doing very well."

"Will you *please* examine the patient?"

He scrubbed up and examined her. "Absolutely a perfect delivery," he said.

The mother left the hospital the eighth day. They named their little boy William Louis.

Shortly after that, I received an invitation from the Board of Directors of Lutheran Hospital, St. Louis, my own school, for the position of director of the school of nursing and nursing service, which I accepted. It was graduation time. The graduation plans and reception plans had been made. On the afternoon of graduation, I invited the graduating class for a conference for anything they might have to bring up or anything they might want to ask.

In came the happy, smiling group of nurses, their hair beautifully groomed to the height of fashion. Before they left, I asked if they always wore their hair that way. They said no. I asked if they were satisfied with their hair that way. They said they were. "I admit it is gorgeous, but I am wondering if the patients you have cared for and the friends you have made during the three years of your student training would not rather see you as they knew you then in your simple and beautiful hairdress."
I blessed them and met them later for the graduating exercise in

the church. Those dear students had redone their hair in the simple and beautiful way they had been accustomed to wearing it.

My years there were happy but very short. I spent most of the evenings standardizing ward service and classroom procedures. Then in 1917, I resigned to go to war.

CHAPTER 5

War Service

In 1916 the War Department ordered six of the large university hospitals to organize complete base hospital units to be ready for overseas service in France when war was declared. These six hospital units were to be loaned to the British government for the duration and were to take over six of their large field hospitals in France. I joined the Washington University unit in St. Louis. Later I learned from the daily paper I was the first Kansan to enlist for war service.

The members of the unit were ordered to be on the alert and ready to move at the moment war was declared. The hospital units were composed of doctors, technicians, corpsmen, dietitians, and nurses. We were ordered to France immediately after war was declared in April, 1917, and landed two weeks later in England. We landed in London, the guests of the city of London, and were royally entertained. Unit one had landed several weeks before. The other units were to follow. General Foch had come from France to meet the units. He brought as a gift a beautiful American flag.

London was a gracious hostess. The highlight of our stay in England, and one which I will always remember, was our investiture by the king, after which we were taken to Saint Paul's Cathedral for the ceremony of the flag. The cathedral was packed when we arrived. The front seats were reserved for the medical and nursing staffs. Some of the doctors and nurses were chosen to sit in the choir loft.

We marched in our full-dress uniforms, sixty-five nurses and forty physicians. When we were all seated, the grand organ struck the notes of that magnificent and majestic hymn "Onward, Christian Soldiers." Everyone rose to his feet immediately. I looked down the large aisle. Standing for a moment at the entrance of the door were the flag-bearers and honor guard bearing our beautiful flag, followed by the battalions, each carrying the flags of their battalions—all singing that majestic hymn "Onward, Christian Soldiers." Everyone in the cathedral was in tears.

The flag-bearer brought the flag to the altar. It was received by the bishop and blessed. The bearers then took the flag to the Hall of Flags to remain there for the duration. It was a gift to our soldiers made by the American and Canadian women living in London with the understanding that at the end of the war it was to be placed in Buckingham Palace, a gift to the king and queen. This was done after the war.

Several years ago when I was in London with friends, we visited Saint Paul's Cathedral. When we entered the cathedral, I burst into tears. I stepped into the etheric record just as it was forty years before.

The next morning we left for Rouen, France. We arrived in the afternoon and marched up the main street, our major and sixty-five nurses each carrying an American flag. We arrived at the hospital about 5:00 p.m. The English were having their farewell tea. They had not expected us until the next morning. There was no preparation for us. The tea broke up. The front was quiet, and we were bedded in patients' beds for the night.

The following morning we rose early for the ceremony of taking over the hospital and the raising of our flag by the side of the British flag at the entrance of the racecourse on which was the large field hospital. The entire units took part in that. Both the American and British units attended. It was a solemn occasion. We became the British Base Hospital number 12 BEF, American Base Hospital number 21 AEF, our insignia during the war. There is nothing in this world which touches the heart so deeply as to see our flag in a foreign country; and nothing can be compared to the feeling of love and admiration and pride, and sadness too, to see the flag over the battlefield. There are no words to describe that feeling.

The hospital was on the racecourse, made up of large open tents. The weather was lovely and we kept them open. There were huts for the seriously wounded and very ill patients.

My first assignment was chief nurse of the medical division. It was a much larger hospital than we expected. The chief nurse sent immediately for forty-five additional graduate nurses. The grandstand could be used for patients if necessary. The corpsmen were a great help.

Soon I was assigned to the operating room. (I had had a course in anesthesia very early in my graduate work to refresh my experience in anesthesia in preparation for going to the front.) Each unit was composed of the surgeon, an assistant, anesthetist, surgical nurse, and the corpsman. Our assignment was for three months. Patients were brought in from the field, operated on, and sent to the base hospitals for further treatment and care; they also carried patients to the boats.

On our return to Rouen, we came through Paris. Walking down one of the boulevards, coming toward us were two medical officers. One was smiling. He was the doctor to whom my sister was engaged. It was a joy to see him. We were on our way to be picked up for our return to Rouen, they on their way to report. We had no time for a visit, nor for a cup of coffee. When we arrived in Rouen, I was appointed night supervisor of the medical division. There was also a night supervisor of the surgical division. One of our duties was to alert the chief nurse of air raids.

I had served as night supervisor for about a month when I was assigned chief nurse of a hospital train. The hospital trains were complete hospitals in every way and could meet and take care of any emergency. The staff consisted of three doctors and three nurses, the surgeon and two assistants, and seventy corpsmen. We had our dining room which served as a recreation room if we wished it. The medical staff had their own area separated from the nurses. We were never permitted to leave the train for any reason. Our duty was to carry sick and wounded to hospitals and ships. There were seventy corpsmen with their separate dining room, which also served as recreation room when there was time. (Three separate units.)

We were not allowed to go out with officers or soldiers from the beginning to the end of the war. I made rounds to get the layout of the train, and on rounds and at night would often stop in the corpsmen's recreation car and spend a few moments with them and in the kitchen to thank the chef. I happened to be fond of raised doughnuts. I asked the chef, a good-natured colored chef, if he could bake doughnuts. He said, "I sure can! Do you like them?" I said, "Yes, I do." He said, "I will be glad to make them for you," and he did, and we enjoyed them. It was an interesting service. Since we were not permitted to leave the train, we were in constant service. The railroad tracks were our garage. We were constantly ready. The engine would be attached to the train, and off we would go for patients.

I remember the chief medical officer left the train on an errand. When he came back, the train was gone. Trains were fully equipped for any emergency or any kind of patient, even a morgue.

Soon after the war was ended, I had a cable from home. My

niece had died. She was my eldest sister's daughter (eighteen years old). Also, mother was not at all well. I had served faithfully. I felt I would like to go home. I called our chief nurse in Paris. She said, "Yes, you may go home, but we have planned to send you to Germany for some special work." I thanked her, but I really felt I wanted to go home. She said: "I am sorry. We had planned on you. I'll send you your discharge in a few days."

In my war service I had not forgotten *Ich Dien*. Life had given us a wonderful opportunity to serve quietly wherever we might be. It was always a joy. We learned much from the sick and wounded—courage, strength, fortitude—and from each other also. *Ich Dien*.

Soon I was on my way home. The hospital train on which I was serving escorted me to the ship—a lone person on a long empty train. They said that was their way of showing their appreciation for my service and to show their thank you.

Nurses were arriving. The ship's railing was lined with naval officers watching the arrivals. Soon we set sail. Then came the commanding officer, second in command, looking for someone. He said to me, "Are you Miss so and so?"

I said, "No, but I will find her for you."

He answered, "No, you're the one we want."

He then said to me that I was to be in charge as chief nurse. I said I would be glad to help, but had been a chief nurse all the way through the war and would just like to be a nurse. I should have known better. He smiled and walked away. Soon he came back with a written order from the captain, and of course that settled it.

Then he suggested that I select three nurses. "The navy will appoint them as your assistant officers of the day. They can take care of the patients and make rounds. You will accompany me on rounds in the morning and evening and be my assistant, and during the day they can report to you." This worked out very satisfactorily.

During this time the corpsmen were permitted to have a dance. That was a real joy for them all. I was with the officers chaperoning when one of the soldiers stepped up to the navy captain and asked him a question. This captain drew himself up in all his dignity and gave him a curt answer.

I asked the captain afterward, "Why did you answer that way?"

He said, "To remind him of his military etiquette."

I said that was too bad. "Those boys have had military discipline for two years. They need kindness and understanding." He did not reply.

Bed patients were getting better, but it was very hot in their bunks. I asked the chief if we might have a large tarpaulin tent put up on the deck and bring up the sickest nurses. They did. He asked me if I were going to sleep on the deck with them. I answered yes, I planned to. It was a godsend; my only regret was for the sick servicemen who could not come up too. After that, recovery was very fast for most of them because of the lovely fresh air. I think we were twelve days coming over.

I was always up early. I was responsible for the three officers of the day (the young nurses), who were enjoying what they were doing. All was well. The morning before we were to land, all the nurses were up early (there were other nurses being released for home beside sick nurses). I sent word to the captain asking if I might have breakfast on deck in the tent this morning. He sent back word, "You already own part of this ship; the rest is yours for the asking." I had a beautiful tray. I could have fed many of the group.

As we were to land the next morning, that day the entire atmosphere of the ship changed and became again a naval activity. The next morning all officers of the ship reported to the captain in full-dress uniform, and I also for the nurses. We received our orders and landed in New York several hours later. My responsibility was to see that the nurses were taken to the nursing center and hospitals, that the well ones reported to headquarters and all had their equipment and baggage. All did have their baggage but me. I stayed over two days. It had not been found. The corpsmen said they would do everything they could to find it. In about two weeks they sent it to me.

At about six o'clock in the afternoon, after having taken care of the nurses in the hospitals and said goodbye to them and after all were properly taken care of in the hotel reserved for nurses, I went to a hotel for the night and left within a few days for my home in Kansas.

The war was over. We never had an air raid at Rouen, although we were alerted several times. I am sure it was because we kept a constant novena in our hearts, a constant faith that every prayer would be answered. God is always where we are and always answers prayers. My life had been dedicated to God, and I lived but for one thing—*Ich Dien*. I trust that in the months of my war service I had brought some comfort and some peace and new faith to the many lives in distress whom I contacted. When there was opportunity, I spoke. Otherwise I was silent. And I trust that I left an imprint on the sands of time.

CHAPTER 6

At Home

I arrived in my home and it seemed so good to be with the family again. It had been many years since I had been home for any length of time. My mother was not very well and asked if I would stay with them one year. This I promised to do.

One evening while mother and I were sitting on the porch, coming down the walk was the chief surgeon of Christ Hospital to see me. I did not know him—only by sight. Mother did. He said he knew I was back and had come to offer me the position of director of nursing service and director of the School of Nursing at Christ Hospital. I told him I would think it over and let him know. It was an answer to prayer and another door of opportunity opened; for with that opportunity I could stay in Topeka, be with the family, and still follow my chosen profession.

I was discharged from the army in August of 1919. Our unit had been decorated by the British government as well as by our own government.

I took charge of Christ Hospital and the School of Nursing in September of 1919. It was a real homecoming. My family lived in Topeka; they were pioneers there, and the years that I spent there were very happy. I was in time to receive the fall class. Christ Hospital was an Episcopal hospital, and there was a cross on top of the chapel.

I remember one student arriving in the evening said to me, "When I saw that cross gleaming in the moonlight, it frightened me a moment; for I felt I was going into a house of God and would there be prepared to serve mankind." This was my object and my purpose: to teach young women to be prepared to be not only professional women, but to be spiritual helpers as well.

Among the applications for the school, we received one from an Indian girl. She wrote that she had written to several hospitals in the East, but the schools would not admit her because she was an Indian. We admitted her. I then called the student body for a conference, read her letter to them, and said, "We admitted her." I knew I could depend on their courtesy and understanding and was sure they would remember the Golden Rule. They did. She was an excellent student, reserved but happy.

The hospital had a beautiful small chapel. We had chapel every morning at six-thirty. A young Episcopal priest served and held the beautiful service of morning prayer. He asked me one morning what I thought of the service. I said: "It is beautiful, but our students come from various denominations. I believe, if you will permit me to say, that a prayer, song, and an inspirational talk on service or talk on ideals of living would help them more than the ritual that they do not understand." He was cooperative and changed the service. I always attended chapel with them.

I was always on duty at 7:00 a.m. to receive the night report from the night supervisor and to make rounds, especially to the very sick and the preoperative and postoperative patients before breakfast. This procedure I followed through the war and my entire hospital and war service. The surgical patients had been given a preoperative medication. Most of them were frightened. It was a wonderful opportunity to say a word to them or just take their hand for a moment. Sometimes I would go into the operating room with them for a moment.

On an occasion we had a desperately ill patient who had been operated on and had to be reoperated on. I went to the operating room and found the surgeon sitting in the doctor's room with his head in his hands. He seemed worried and distressed. I sat down beside him and said: "You seem worried. Would you like me to offer a prayer for you and for the patient?"

He shook his head yes.

Then I asked, "Would you like me to come to the operating room for a few moments?"

"Yes."

I went into the operating room and stayed a few moments. The patient, very ill, made a good recovery. It was the surgeon's skill, but it was also our faith and prayer.

My mother suddenly took a turn for the worse. I brought her to the hospital so she could receive the very best of care. The doctors were very attentive to her, as were the nurses, but she was unconscious and never regained consciousness. She passed away the evening before the graduation.

I knew what graduation means to student nurses; and I knew, too, that I would not spoil their graduation. I called the graduating class together and told them we would carry on just as we had planned. I would be going home that night, but would return the following morning at ten o'clock to carry on.

The hospital was centered in several acres of beautiful grounds and trees, and I had planned for them a graduation at sundown. The sunsets in Kansas are magnificent. I asked the bishop if we could have the cathedral choir, the churchwardens, and of course himself in the procession. I had asked the medical staff to be in the procession also. He said they would be happy to do it, as was the medical staff.

Mother passed away at six o'clock in the evening before the graduation, too late to get the notice in the paper that night. The graduation the next night was just at sundown, too early for most people to have read it that night, so there was no sadness or sympathy about the graduation at all. It was a beautiful sight—the cathedral choir, the medical staff, the graduates, the student nurses, the churchwardens, and the bishop. We sat facing the audience. When I looked up and saw my mother's closest friend sitting as far front as she could, I knew why she had come. But I knew I had no right to dim this beautiful affair or the joy of the graduates by even a thought or tear of sadness. Just as the sun was sinking, they were consecrated and dedicated. The singing of the magnificent Lord's Prayer closed the ceremony. There was a huge audience and it was a beautiful affair.

In those days dances were often held out of doors on platforms built on the lawn, and we had planned also to have a dance after the graduation ceremony. I stayed with them until ten o'clock, then left them in the hands of others and went home.

I found the home full of beautiful flowers. My mother's funeral was private. A day or two after the funeral, I went back to the hospital and carried on.

In 1920, the now world-famous Dr. Karl Menninger, psychiatrist, the son of Dr. C. F. Menninger, prominent internist of Topeka, had finished his medical training and graduate work in psychiatry and came home to Topeka to set up his practice. His father was the chief internist of our medical staff. He was the one who convinced mother that I be permitted to take up nursing. Dr. Menninger, Sr. was a great inspiration to me all through my life. Dr. Karl Menninger's mother was a great Bible student who established and organized the Menninger Bible Study Class. Dr. Menninger, Sr. gave me as a gift, when I entered training, a beautiful book of inspirational poems, and told me to use it every day. I used it and wore it out!

Dr. Karl asked me if he might set up a hydrotherapy department at Christ Hospital to get started. The large ward on the second floor over the chapel and administrative offices seemed suitable for that service. He was given permission. He started with one patient and one graduate nurse. I am happy that I was a part of his beginning. We have been very close friends ever since.

Shortly after that I received a telegram from the Rockefeller Foundation asking me to come to New York for an interview. I had been recommended for a position in Brazil. The Rockefeller Foundation had a tremendous program in public health and education under the International Health Board of the Rockefeller Foundation in South America, especially Brazil. In a few days I left for New York for the interview.

The interview lasted a week. I was interviewed by the directors and the heads of the departments. Always there were one of their staff and a secretary who sat in on the interview. Each interview lasted the better part of a day. It was thorough, very interesting, and so diplomatically done that one hardly realized it was an interview.

At the end of the week I was to meet the president of the foundation. He informed me that I had been chosen for the position in Brazil. I thanked him and said, "I am so grateful the interviews are over."

"Was it as bad as that?"

"No, it was not bad; but it was really a strain and I knew what was being done. But it was so graciously done I really did not mind."

He asked me how soon I could be ready, and I replied that I would report as soon as I could fill my position and the new director was oriented. This was satisfactory to him.

Then he asked if there was anything they could do to help me before I left. I asked him if I might have a traveling fellowship to visit several large hospitals—one university hospital, one large general hospital, and one private hospital. University schools of nursing were just being organized, and I wanted to familiarize myself with the organization and the program since I was to organize the program in connection with the University of Brazil for the Brazilian government.

He asked me to select the schools. I selected Yale University Hospital, Massachusetts General Hospital, and Saint Luke's Hospital in New York. I spent two weeks in each hospital; it was an interesting and satisfying experience, and I was greatly enriched by it. I knew, too, that going to a foreign country with a foreign language where there was no knowledge of modern nursing would be a challenge and would need more than nursing. The president asked me to telephone every day to let them know how I was getting along and if there was anything I might be wanting. I did call them every day.

Again the door had been opened. I was unafraid. I knew the Hand that had led me thus far would lead me through. The position for which I had been accepted was that of organizing a modern school of nursing, one on the university level, in connection with the University of Brazil for the Brazilian government. Modern nursing was unknown in Brazil. But my faith in God was unquestioned.

I was given the opportunity to select my staff of graduates and to take them with us when we left. I selected only one. She was a mature, well-balanced, experienced nurse. I did not select the others. I wanted to see the setup, to meet officers of the hospital and university, to know a little of the people, to know what would be expected of us.

Finally the day arrived for our departure, and that morning a breakfast was given for the seventeen of us. The director of the International Public Health Program and the director of the International Education Program for South America were accompanying us to Rio de Janeiro. The others were going to other parts of Brazil. The president's last words to me were "Miss Kieninger, the Rockefeller Foundation bet every dollar they have on you."

I answered, "Thank you, I shall try not to disappoint you."

CHAPTER 7

Brazil

We were fifteen days journeying to South America. They were delightful days. We arrived in Rio de Janeiro and were royally received and royally entertained. Mrs. Parsons, who had preceded me for her public health work, the two directors from the foundation, the director of public health, the director of education, and I were the guests of honor. Present were the minister of public health, the minister of education, Dr. Strode, the head of the Rockefeller Foundation in Brazil, our ambassador, and several others.

The next morning we were taken to the hospital. It is on the Mangue (a canal through the middle of the street), on each side a row of royal palms. It is a beautiful hospital surrounded with a wall and a large iron door at the entrance. It is in the shape of a six-pointed star, each point a large ward independent of the next ward, opening onto a large round tile patio. The wards were also tile.

On the first floor were the business offices and two very large offices for the school of nursing, all tile. My office was completely furnished. Later we equipped the second office with mimeograph machines, typewriters, and desks and tables. There were no nursing books, and all books had to be translated.

I asked the administrator to secure a young woman with

business training and experience. I interviewed her and tagged her for later. She knew mimeographing, which was important. She was a Barbadian, knew English, and was a well-trained secretary —a real joy.

The first floor was reserved for men, the large clinic, and the x-ray department. The second floor was reserved for women and children and operating rooms. The wards all had large French windows that were never closed.

The hospital had been dedicated years before to São Francesco de Assisi (the master Kuthumi). It bears his name. It is the teaching hospital for doctors, medical and nursing students.

As soon as the foundation directors returned to the States, I went to Teresopolis, a summer resort high in the mountains, to live with a Brazilian family who could not read or speak a word of English. I, of course, could not read or speak Portuguese. Brazil is the only country in South America in which the Portuguese language is spoken. Portugal conquered Brazil in the eighteenth century. Soon the Brazilians revolted and drove out the king and queen. When the queen embarked on the ship which was to take her back to Portugal, she took off her shoes, threw them into the bay, and said, "I will not take even the dust of Brazil to my country."

The assistant of the minister of public health was appointed administrator of the hospital temporarily. Dr. Strode was available; it was nice to know he was so interested. As soon as the budget was passed, they notified me and I returned from Teresopolis to start the program (I had been gone one month).

The administrator of the hospital was a rather young man, very cooperative and helpful in every way. We worked together in perfect harmony. He was patient, kind, never too busy to help or advise in any way. It was a pleasure to work with him.

The hospital wards were not equipped with anything but beds, bedside tables, chairs, mattresses on the beds, and pillows.

There was no ready-made hospital linen available. Everything for the hospital had to be made. Fortunately the Singer Sewing Machine Company had an agency in Rio, and we rented ten sewing machines from them. I asked the administrator to buy bolts of muslin, gauze, etc., and also to get twenty seamstresses for us. Brazilian women use their hands very well and are excellent with the needle. Fortunately I had selected as my assistant a middle-aged nurse with practical as well as hospital experience. She certainly proved her worth.

I chose to select my own staff in Brazil. I chose only one nurse in New York. I wanted to meet university faculty as well as hospital staff to find out what they expected of us. Fortunately I had not selected the others. There were a number of graduate nurses in Rio. I was delighted. I interviewed them and I was more delighted. They had personality, maturity, and experience. They had been pioneers, which was a great help. They knew the language more or less. Two were from England, one from Norway, one from Holland. I had them appointed on the staff.

Then I met an American nurse who was visiting her sister's family, and I asked her to join our staff. She also had an excellent nursing background. She did but said it would have to be temporary, but she stayed on. Later I met a very fine American nurse born and reared in Brazil and educated in the United States who had just graduated with her B.S. in nursing and returned to Rio. She was happy to join our staff. I was delighted with them—seven well-balanced, mature, dependable, experienced nurses. I had them appointed at once on our staff. Two were to follow as soon as they had graduated from a university and received their B.S. in nursing. I was happy indeed and very grateful. Again, the Light of God never fails.

I had asked for several long tables to be set up in one of the wards and asked the supervising staff if they would supervise the making of sheets, pillow slips, towels, etc., and showed them how to make supplies for the operating rooms, clinic, and wards. It was a very busy time, but it was a happy one too.

The wards had to be set up; operating room, clinics, utility and dressing rooms had to be made ready, students interviewed, classroom for the emergency course equipped. This room was made ready immediately for the group who would be admitted shortly.

The *madama* (housekeeper), a German widow of a government employee, was most efficient. The hospital, all windows and tile, was easy to keep immaculate and was always that way. The employed Brazilian women were excellent seamstresses. They worked ten hours a day. We served them breakfast, lunch, and coffee several times a day. The graduates enjoyed that particular service very much.

Then there was the problem of getting an educational director who could speak and teach in Portuguese. That was imperative. Great is the love and power of God! I met the much-loved American missionary who had been in Brazil since his youth. He told me he had a daughter studying nursing in one of the university schools in the United States and that she would receive her B.S. degree in several months. I asked him if she had plans and he replied "None." She was returning home to Rio.

I wrote to her, offering her the position as my assistant in charge of the educational program and also that the Rockefeller Foundation would grant her a fellowship. I suggested that if she take it, she make it soon. We needed her very much. Also, would she select a graduate from her school? She could help in the classroom in teaching nursing procedures. It would simplify the teaching of nursing procedures if teachers were from the same school.

I then presented the nursing staff to the medical and surgical staff of the hospital. We discussed supplies and asked for their suggestions and for anything they might wish; supplies were uniform. The medical staff was delighted and we established excellent rapport. Then we arranged conferences with the chiefs of the staff of operating room and clinic to meet the charge nurses to see if they had any particular wishes for supplies or anything they might wish to discuss. The operating staff had only a few specialties.

The time was drawing near when patients would be admitted. There was no one to take care of them. I asked the administrator if he would secure twenty-five or thirty young Brazilian women for interview and told him what we wanted them for.

In the meantime Mrs. Parsons, the director of the public health nursing program, had stabilized her staff. When she and her six graduate public health nurses arrived, they found well technically trained young Brazilian women in the health department, but they had no nursing background. I called Mrs. Parsons to tell her we had planned to set up an emergency course of three months—classes in practical nursing to train young Brazilian women to work as ward helpers, to assist in the wards until our students had passed the preclinical courses and could be placed on the wards to remain as ward helpers. I had interviewed twenty-five young Brazilian women.

Would she be interested in having her lay group get some practical bedside nursing experience? If so, would she lend us two of her graduate supervisors to assist with teaching? If so, we would include technique for home care and one month's experience on the ward. This she was willing to do. I asked her if she would like to interview any of the young women. She said she would like to send some of her lay staff. This course was set up immediately. It would serve two purposes: to prepare ward assistants for our wards and to give the lay personnel some bedside nursing experience.

In less then two weeks we admitted thirty-five young Brazilian women for the emergency course; two public health nurses and one of the hospital supervisors taught. Classes were begun at once. Hospital supervisors were sterilizing supplies for operating room, clinic, and wards and getting the wards ready for patients.

I was interviewing young women for the school. Next to the hospital was a two-story building for the student nurses' home—a wall on one side, the hospital on the other. It had a very large room, kitchen, and dining room and a very large patio on the ground floor. The very large room lent itself very well for the nursing classroom and other classes. We had it completely equipped. The second floor had a small drawing room, bedrooms, and a small room for study. The patio was beautiful and large. We had all of our meals out of doors. The graduate staff had their meals with us. It was delightful. We had an opening made in the wall between hospital and home. The patio lent itself very well for any fiestas we might have. It had large iron doors at the entrance.

During this time the hospital had been officially opened. It was a joyous and proud moment—a beautiful hospital, everything new and shining. It had been blessed by the priest. Dignitaries of the government and university, Dr. Chagas, the eminent scientist, the medical staff, and many others were present. They were shown through the hospital. All were delighted. Patients would be coming in within a few days. The nursing staff were the hostesses; coffee was served.

Even before the hospital was officially opened, we had opened the children's ward. Thirty children were transferred from one of the hospitals. One of the children died. I went immediately to the administrator to report it. He said, "It will be taken care of."

I asked, "Do you call the priest?"

He said, "Priest?"

"Do you notify the family?"

He said: "Senhora, the mother of that child does not know

where that child is. There is no priest necessary; but if you want one, I will call him."

I answered, "Yes, I think I do."

He called one.

The child had a Christian burial. I suddenly realized that it was not a Catholic hospital. It was the university hospital, a teaching hospital to teach doctors, interns, medical students, and nursing students. I came to teach and to learn, and gratefully I learned to adjust myself to the ways of the people. It was a pleasure. We established a happy relationship. Within a few days the hospital was completely filled with patients.

The emergency class was just about finished and students were ready for wards. We had a celebration. Flowers were arriving, as were guests: Mrs. Parsons and staff, Dr. Chagas, the minister of education, the minister of public health, and staff members of the hospital and public health. We gave the public health students arm bands with the letters "V.S.P. (Visitadores de Saúde Pública).

Just before the end of the ceremony, an easel was brought in draped in Brazilian and American flags. When it was unveiled, it was my picture, which they had enlarged and beautifully framed. It was a complete surprise. You can imagine my feeling. Before I left Brazil, I had many occasions to know the warmth of the hearts of those blessed Brazilians—loyal, faithful, and generous. D. Laura, as usual, had a beautiful supper prepared. It was a solemn and happy and proud occasion. Next morning they were placed on the wards.

Doctors came into the wards to congratulate them and drink coffee to them. They were faithful and loyal workers "for God and my country." After a month's service on the wards, the public health students returned to the health department. It was successful. We thought we might repeat it later to give all in the public health nursing department an experience in nursing until graduates of the school could take it over. (Some of our graduating students took their scholarships in the United States in public health.)

In interviewing young women for the school, I found that about half of them would not be permitted to sleep away from their homes. We named them *externato;* the students who came into the home we named *internato.* Too, the home was just big enough for the students accepted. Later the government secured a lovely large home on a half-acre of ground near a small hill, all enclosed with a wall, large iron doors at the entrance. Before the second class was admitted we moved the first class into it. We kept the original one for new students. We secured a bus to carry students to and from the hospital, and a very large beautiful dog. The chauffeur also acted as houseman. All students had lunch at the original home. In six weeks all students were permitted to come in. We had proven ourselves.

The Opening of School

It was an exciting time. We did not have a celebration. Parents were welcome to come to see us and see where their daughters would live. Miss Lander and assistant had arrived. We had set up the curriculum and were busy translating nursing textbooks.

The next morning I presented the students to the nursing faculty, then opened the school with the orientation class, and we discussed the ideals of nursing—what others could expect from us and what we would expect of them. There were questions—anything they wished to bring up at that time. They were from convent schools and a real joy. They were happy they would be serving "God and their fellowman." They chose to have a student government. It was a delightful class "for God and our country and fellowman."

There were no discipline problems at any time as far as the

school was concerned. If they had any, they were among themselves. The only real problems I remember they had were after they received their caps. One student, a foreigner (whose parents were very highly respected and prominent in Brazil), came home one afternoon with her hair bobbed. It was the time when women were beginning to bob their hair. They were pretty excited about it. They asked me what would we do about it. I said it is too late to do anything about it. Let us practice the Golden Rule. She is the only foreigner (her family lives in São Paulo) in a group of closely knit friends and probably feels alone and in a moment of homesickness had her hair bobbed. Let us put ourselves in her place; let us ignore it and be gracious and understanding. They did. They did not like to see their cap on a bobbed head. (I did not either, but I did not say so.)

In the group were four students advanced in years and experience. They were a joy and wonderful help for the younger students and for all. D. Laura, our *madama* (housemother), was a refined and lovely person—a disciplinarian with grace and love and a tremendous help to all.

The next morning classes began in nursing technique. Science classes would begin two weeks later. They were taught by professors and medical staff. It was a joy to watch the students. There was no task too great or too small. They expressed inner joy. Everything for God and their beloved country.

Capping

When the students had finished the preclinical period and passed all the examinations, they were ready for their caps. What excitement and happiness! The caps were blessed, pinned on those precious heads in the presence of their families and friends. Members of the nursing profession revere their caps. We taught the students respect for uniforms and caps—never to wear them off the campus, nor their uniforms on the street, but to hold them sacred. The patio was full of beautiful flowers, and Dona Laura had prepared a lovely coffee for the new students and their friends and families. Many of the dignitaries were present also. Flowers were everywhere—a happy and blessed occasion.

The next morning we placed them on the wards. What excitement! Coffee was served to the doctors and others who came into the wards to congratulate them.

One of the lovely customs in Rio is the sending of flowers. Rio de Janeiro is a garden of beautiful flowers of all descriptions, and on the slightest occasion the people send baskets and baskets of flowers. I remember my first birthday in Rio. It was on a Sunday. I had been with friends for dinner; and when I arrived home that evening, on my table was a magnificent large black enamel vase containing a large shower of small yellow orchids from the students.

Our ward helpers who graduated did not receive certificates. They stayed with us as ward helpers, and we felt that every ward helper or every person that we could train or help would be of help to the health of Brazil.

What an opportunity pioneering is! Especially in a foreign country. I did not know Mother Mary then, nor the great masters, but I learned later to know them and to love them. But I loved the Brazilians and in my travels learned to love God's family no matter who or where or what they were. Surely life is a boomerang. What one sends out, good or bad, returns, good or bad. In early life I had learned the Golden Rule.

Our ethical conferences were a joy. The Brazilians have a deep love for their country and a deep love for their fellowmen and a deep respect for elderly people. Surely one could say, even of those young students, "I am my brother's keeper." There was nothing, no task too menial or too difficult to ask of them; nothing was ever too much for them. They were doing it in God's name and for His sake and for Mother Mary's sake. It was a joy to be privileged to associate with them. Their lives were consecrated and dedicated and they lived it. There was never a disciplinary problem as far as the school office was concerned. If they had any, Dona Laura and they cleared them up. There was student government and they governed well. If there were any problems, they were usually among themselves.

The hospital is a government hospital, and there were no shrines or statues of beloved Mother Mary. The students asked me if they might put up a shrine or statue to beloved Mother Mary. I was happy, for I had missed it too. Joyously they arranged a beautiful shrine on which they placed a beautiful statue of Mother Mary on the second floor of the hospital. It was a great blessing and comfort for the patients and the nurses and all. It was a great privilege to be associated with such devoted students.

The YWCA

The YWCA had a well-established organization. It was a very highly respected center. One day the secretary called to ask if I could help her. A Russian artist had come into the office and was looking for help. He had fled from Russia to South America shortly after the Russian Revolution and landed in Rio. He was the portrait painter for the Czar. I told her I would try to do what I could to help him and to send him along.

Soon he arrived with an American interpreter. He spoke no English, Portuguese, German, or French. When I invited them into my office, he was straight as an arrow, clicked his heels, and saluted me. But I could see he was distressed; my heart went out to him, a stranger in a strange country looking for a place to land and to reestablish himself. I put out my hand to make him feel at ease. He took it and touched it with his lips. I do know about human kindness and what it can do for one. The interpreter explained the troubles. I told him I would do what I could, gave him the names of certain of my Brazilian and American friends. I told him I would call them. When I called, they said they would be glad to help him.

In about two months he came again, this time to express his gratitude. He had been well received and had a number of orders. He had come to pay his respects and to do my portrait! I told him I would not have my portrait done. He expressed his thanks over and over and over again, and I expressed mine to him for the opportunity of helping him. When I again refused to have my portrait done, he asked if I did not have someone in the family whose portrait I would like. I had a picture of mother at the age of sixteen; it was my favorite picture of her. I brought it to him and he copied it. It is a beautiful and exquisite treasure. Then he asked if I had someone else, and I said no, that I did not. He said, "You *must* have." I thought of my niece's picture—I had a very beautiful niece. He did that, and it, too, is a beautiful treasure.

When he came back and asked again would I have my portrait painted, I refused again; but his gratitude touched my heart. I never saw him again after that, but my friends reported how satisfied and how grateful they were for my having referred him to them.

Christmas

Christmas is a very sacred season in South America. Every home has a crèche with a beautiful Christ Child. In the homes that can afford it, the Christ Child is dressed gorgeously in the finest silks and laces; in the poorer homes it is dressed very simply, but loved deeply. Every home has one.

The students were all permitted to go home for Christmas, leaving the nurses' home the evening of December 23 after duty. They had decorated the shrine of Mother Mary in the patio. The supervisors alternated Christmas and New Year's. The ward helpers alternated Christmas and New Year's also.

Brazil

I did not go out until dinner on Christmas. When I opened the door on Christmas morning there were several dozen pairs of shoes in front of my door. That is a Christmas custom in Brazil. The shoes are placed there for gifts from the Christ Child. However, I was prepared. Dona Laura, our matron, had warned me of the custom; and I had bought a gift for each one, wrapped them in Christmas paper and bows, and placed them in the shoes. When the students came home about eight o'clock Christmas night, they came to see if there were gifts. They were certainly surprised to find gifts in them! They stood outside my door and sang Christmas songs. It brought much joy for them and for me. Mother Mary's shrine in the patio was beautifully bedecked with flowers.

We had visiting hours in the hospital twice a week, Wednesdays and Sundays, in the afternoon from two to four. Visitors were permitted on Christmas and New Year's. Our hospital was a teaching hospital, and the patients were of the poorer class.

One day Dona Lais, the president of the student body, asked me to come with her to the sculptor. He was sculpturing a bust of me from a picture, and there were some things for which he wanted to see me for a sitting before finishing. The bust was to be a complete surprise; I was not to know anything about it until it was complete, but the sculptor had requested to see me. Had I known of it, I would never have permitted it. My bust and the bust of the famous scientist of Brazil, Dr. Carlos Chagas, also the plaque dedicated to Mrs. Parsons, director of public health nursing, were to be placed in the nurses' home. They were entwined with flowers and flags so that one could hardly see them. The school was the idol, the ideal, and the vision of Dr. Carlos Chagas. He sponsored it, he honored it, and he protected it when it needed protection; and it was in gratitude that the bust was dedicated to him.

The unveiling of the busts and plaque was a brilliant affair, as are all of their affairs. Flowers were sent from everywhere, so profuse we could hardly see each other. (This was in 1925 and the year for the graduation of the first class.)

Social Life

The students were not permitted to entertain men friends in the home. There was much entertaining officially, in which the students were always included and in which government officials often participated. We were often honored by the presence of some representative of the president. The school was becoming the darling of the gods and has remained so to this day. They had kept the high ideals and standards set for them, and today the school is the mother house of nursing, the model for all schools, the head and leader in nursing education, not only for Brazil, but for all of South America. The school was named for Anna Nery, the pioneer volunteer nurse of Brazil, the first woman who volunteered in the first Brazilian war. The students selected the Florence Nightingale lamp as their insignia and the Maltese cross in a circle of gold as their school pin.

One day I asked the students if they would like a picnic. "What's a picnic?" said they. I said, "Let's have one, and you will find out." We selected a beautiful moonlit night, invited the interns and some medical students and Dona Laura. She had a lunch prepared for us, although it was really a dinner. She went with us and we started out. There was much excitement. We went to a small park on a beautiful lake. It was a beautiful night—much happiness, boat riding, and eating. It was a really lovely affair. After the last boat ride, we turned our way home. Everyone asked that we have another picnic soon. The doctors enjoyed it as much as the students.

I felt that the students should have some social activities before their graduation and consulted our patroness, Madame Mesquite, one of the first ladies of Brazil, the social leader interested in the development of Brazilian women in church and politics and in expanding the activities of the women of Brazil at a time when they were not too interested in being expanded. We decided on a social dance. The grounds of the nurses' home were large and beautiful and lent themselves on the lovely lawn very well to an affair such as this. A platform was built for dancing. Interns, medical students, and friends and families of the students were invited. They were well chaperoned. It was a beautiful affair on a brilliant moonlit night, and the happiness of the students was a joy to see.

When I was in Rio in 1942 to help them set up their defense war program, I met many of the medical group again. Several doctors said to me: "We remember how delightful was the graduation dance and how you circled among us, especially when we were sitting out. Gracious you were, but we knew what you were doing."

I asked them, "What was I doing? Did you approve?"

"Yes, we approved, and we approve it more now."

The second large affair was the reception given by Madame Mesquite in her beautiful villa. The honor guests were the four graduates who would be leaving right after the graduation for the United States. In the receiving line were the four honor students; Dr. Chagas, the eminent scientist; Dr. Strode, the head of the Rockefeller Foundation for Brazil; a representative of the president of Brazil; our ambassador, Mr. Morgan; Mrs. Parsons, and I. It was a brilliant affair.

The third large affair was on the morning of the graduation. The entire student body and I were taken to the Candelabra Cathedral for the blessing of the caps which would be worn that night at the graduation and for taking pictures of it. It was a joyous, holy, and beautiful service.

We had our usual lovely luncheon in the home by our beloved *madama,* D. Laura. The day was full of excitement, and the happiness and joy of the students was wonderful to see.

The graduation was held that night in the exclusive and charming club De Flamengo. The club was packed. The student body had marched in earlier and taken their places on the platform. When the grand pipe organ began the magnificent march, "Festival Overture" by Guilmant, everyone was standing. The graduating class and faculty marched to the platform. On the platform awaiting the graduating class was the bishop; to his right were Dr. Carlos Chagas and Mr. Morgan, American ambassador; and to his left were Dr. Strode and the representative of the president of Brazil. Mrs. Parsons took her place on the right of Mr. Morgan. I took mine on the left of the representative of the president. It was a beautiful and sacred service and graduation, the fulfillment of Dr. Chagas's dream. His happiness and pride were a joy to see and were shared by all of Brazil.

The school was sound and well established and accepted by the university and government of Brazil. The staff was stable. The four honor students were off to the United States on scholarships. Books were being written and translated. A second class had been accepted and admitted. It was only the beginning of a brilliant future for the school and for its graduates and for the young women of Brazil. I had requested that I might be released after the first class graduated. It had been a happy five years.

The door that opened to me then has never been closed. It is as wide open now as it was then, and it was twenty-seven years ago that I was asked to come to Brazil again to help set up their war defense program for the lay group and nurses. The door will be open through all eternity.

The American colony once asked me why I paid so little attention to the Americans in Brazil, and I answered: "I have 120 million Americans at home. I know Americans, but I do not know the Brazilians. I came to bring our culture to them; but I came also to learn their culture, their country, their people, and to help their young women to fulfill their divine plan in their way and in their culture. I love Brazil; I love her and her people."

Departure

The time had arrived for my departure. Gifts were flowing in from everywhere—laces, linens, jewelry, silver, treasures of all kinds. The linens and laces and jewelry were exquisite. Telegrams and flowers were profuse.

I did not go to the States immediately. Somehow I could not. I took a freighter around South America, through the Magellan Strait, up the west coast of South America, and through the Panama Canal. The ship was anchored in the bay; we were to sail at six o'clock. There were more gifts and flowers everywhere. As the anchor was released, I stood by the railing to wave goodbye. There were many at the dock to see me off. The entire student body, government officials, doctors, friends, and flowers. They had built a table which was laden with gifts. The gifts I appreciated most were the beautiful Brazilian flag which they had made for me in a box made of the woods of Brazil lined with cream velvet and a small flag to carry with me.

As I left the platform to embark, the students burst into the school song; the water was covered with flowers. Fortunately we started out almost immediately. Nurses and friends were waving American and Brazilian flags and throwing flowers into the water. I knew then that I was leaving part of my heart in Brazil.

It is still there.

Night comes suddenly in the tropics. I stood at the stern of the ship to wave goodbye. I stayed there until the lights of Brazil faded from the coast. Only the light on the statue of Christ of Corcovado was still visible, and soon that, too, faded into the night. I stood there a few minutes longer watching the stars which seemed almost like suns. It was a beautiful night. Then I turned and went into my cabin for the night.

In the morning I met the other guests on the ship; two English families from Patagonia were returning from England from the graduation of their sons at Oxford. There were ten of us counting the children. They were delightful people. The sea was calm and the day perfect. We remained in Patagonia two days. Stopping at the port of call was a delightful break in the journey.

The weather was changing and the sea was getting rough as we neared Patagonia, where the passengers disembarked. We took no passengers from there, and I was the only passenger until we came to the Panama Canal.

The sea was getting very rough before we entered the straits, and it certainly was rough while we were in the straits. Everything on the ship had been tied down. I went into my cabin with orders not to leave it for twenty-four hours. I thought I might have to be tied in my bed; but tall boards had been put up, and even though I rolled, I managed to stay in.

By the next day we were through the worst, although the sea was still very rough. But it was calming and the sun was shining. I was not then or at any other time seasick. It was an experience I was glad to have had but am happy I shall never have again.

The ship's crew were wonderful men. When we stopped at ports of call, the natives would come in their rowboats laden with wares. I bought a lovely round basket with a top to carry some of the gifts I had received at the boat. The crew boxed the other gifts I had received at the boat. I enjoyed every minute of that beautiful voyage.

The journey through the Panama Canal was delightful, and soon afterwards we landed in New York. In four months of delightful sea travel, I had encircled South America. I stopped in every country and traveled almost fifteen thousand miles (14,976 to be exact) by water from New York to New York.

I expected to leave for home the evening after landing in New York after a brief visit to the Rockefeller Foundation. However, the next morning while I was at breakfast at the International House, two young women came to my table. They were in tears when they saw me. They were honor students who had come up from Brazil just a few weeks before on scholarships; and they were homesick, alone, and afraid. They had started their English classes. They asked me how long I would be there, and I replied that I was leaving that evening for home. "Please, please stay with us today," they pleaded. I told them I had an appointment that afternoon for a tea honoring my return. However, I phoned the foundation. The president had been in Brazil, as had some of the other officers. They knew of my work and also knew of my leaving. Therefore I was excused from reporting to the foundation, and I stayed with the Brazilian students until four o'clock. My train left at five.

CHAPTER 8

Denver

About a month after I arrived home, a friend wrote of a temporary position at the University of Colorado School of Nursing in Denver. I was interested. I wrote and received a reply asking me to send a photograph. In a short time I was appointed to the position of Director of the School of Nursing and director of nursing of Colorado General and Colorado Psychopathic Hospitals. I arrived on the appointed day in September of 1926, in time for the opening of the fall term. The education director was on her vacation. I had the opportunity to get acquainted with the nursing and teaching staff and the hospital staff. The position was temporary for three or four months only. The present director had had surgery and was on a three-month leave of absence. The School of Nursing and the School of Medicine are on the Denver campus, as are the general and psychopathic hospitals. The other schools are in Boulder.

Near the end of three months, the administrator asked me to come to his office. He offered me the position permanently. I asked him if the director of the school had resigned. He replied no. I asked him if she was coming back, and he said he didn't know. I told him I would consider staying only until she returned. I felt that as long as she had been ill and had been granted a leave of absence by the university and had not resigned, I could not and would not accept the position. If she were not yet able to come back, I would remain until she was able to return. I felt it was not honorable to take a position of a person while she was ill or on a convalescent leave of absence. I said: "How do I know but what in a few months you would treat me the same way? I would not like it, and I am sure she would not like it nor would you."

Soon the president of the university was announced and came into my office. He said, "Miss ——— has resigned." I asked him if she had been asked to resign and he replied no. Then I told him how I felt about accepting the position, that I had no baccalaureate degree and felt the director of the school of nursing of a university should have one, which of course he already knew. The hospital was fairly new and the school had recently been transferred from the Boulder Hospital. He said, "You have the qualities we need, and that is more important." It was important perhaps at that time.

I finally accepted the position and told him I would remain until they could find some suitable person who qualified for the position and who had at least a B.S., preferably an M.A. degree. This was in the summer of 1926. I stayed until 1941, fifteen years—fifteen happy years.

Depression—1932

During the depression in 1932, when even nurses were without employment and often in need, the Colorado State Nurses Association appointed a committee to study the nursing situation and find ways and means to help them. As a result of that study, the committee made the following recommendations: that hospitals employ graduate nurses on a half-time basis four hours a day, six days a week, with two meals, at fifty dollars per month and that the two universities accept graduates thus employed on half-time basis for classes without tuition. These recommendations were adopted by the hospitals and the two universities, Colorado University in Boulder and Denver University in Denver. We chose Denver University, as the nurses lived in Denver. The University of Colorado is in Boulder, and there would be the transportation problem. Many graduates took advantage of the university offer and after the depression continued their studies and graduated with a B.S. in nursing.

Denver 1930

The nursing project worked out very well. Only those employed in hospitals on a half-time basis were given the opportunity of attending the university free. I had been thinking what opportunities we could offer WPA workers and discussed this with the hospital administrator and with the nursing faculty. All approved. I called the administrator of the WPA and offered our help. He asked me how many we could use. I said one hundred. He asked me again. I said one hundred.

"A hundred? What will you do with a hundred?"

"Put them to work!"

By the time they were weeded out, there would not be that many. The WPA director had the same reaction as the administrator of the hospital—surprised but very happy. Then I called the nursing faculty, and we discussed plans and ways we could use them.

We did not assign any of the WPA workers to the psychopathic hospital, but to the general hospital only. These were the conditions we set up: that an office be set up for the project with its own supervisor in the basement of the hospital (ground floor);

that the WPA supervisor handle any and all disciplinary problems; that he keep the time book; that the workers report to him off and on duty (their hours of duty would be 7:00 to 2:00 and 2:00 to 9:00; we reestablished the hours when and if necessary); that he report any absence to the nursing supervisor. They would be eligible to our clinics if they were ill.

I also asked that we appoint a graduate nurse supervisor for them. She was a member of our staff. In this way there was rapport, and good working relationships were retained. The graduate supervisor was responsible for them and worked in rapport with the instructor on the wards. We placed them on the wards, in the supply rooms, in the linen rooms, in the dining rooms, wherever they were needed. They did not replace anyone employed; they were added help.

The program worked out very well. As I remember, there were no disciplinary problems. If they were inadequate for the work, the supervisor of the project replaced them. During that period several government officials probably on their regular inspection tours inspected the program and gave us a very high rating.

I remember well the morning they reported for duty. There were a hundred of them. They were sitting in the amphitheater of the medical school, awaiting us, at eight o'clock in the morning. I introduced the nursing faculty to them and then told them what we would expect of them and what they could expect of us. It was, as far as we were concerned and as far as the WPA was concerned, a very successful project. It also prepared them for their future.

Some of our medical students worked on the wards for their meals. We discussed giving them some of the nurses' classes in procedures if they wished it. The dean and the medical school faculty approved. This, I remember, was an elective course. Colorado was at that time more of a rural state, and we thought many of our medical students should probably practice in some of the smaller towns and villages and that probably some of the nursing procedures would be helpful to them. In pediatrics we taught them to care for premature babies, also how to set up an incubator. The medical students were appreciative and it was a success. We taught them any special procedures they wished to know.

Conferences

Our nursing faculty met once a week. There was nothing too great or too small for us to discuss and adopt if approved. There was perfect rapport. Any policy, any problems were discussed, and we welcomed any suggestions from the medical staff and even the student nurses. The head nurses met every two weeks, and their suggestions and discussion of their problems and difficulties were always welcome. Some of them were excellent. We discussed them in faculty and adopted them if approved. In this way there was uniformity in the hospitals. The nurses made a fine contribution to the success of the program.

All students accepted in the school were given a physical examination in our clinic before they were finally accepted. Although a physical examination was required for entrance to the school, we had the students examined after they were admitted.

On one occasion during the physical examination of the students, the intern came into the office to report that one of the young women was pregnant. I asked him to send her to me. Into the office came a beautiful young woman. I asked her to sit down and said: "The doctor tells me you are pregnant. Did you know it?"

She said, "Yes, but I did not know it until he told me."

She was from a western state, graduated from the University of Colorado, and decided to take up nursing. She said: "I do not know what I will do. I don't want my family to know I am pregnant."

I asked her if she would like me to help her.

She was grateful and said, "Would you?"

I wanted to send her to the Salvation Army Hospital (our interns served there), but she had friends among the students. It would be better to send her where they could not contact her. There was another maternity home for unwed girls in Denver. I had not met the matron, but I called her and asked if she would take this young woman and explained the circumstances. After a little while she said, "I will take her, but you (meaning me) cannot come to see her; you cannot call her by phone or write to her." I said, "I'll obey your rules; you can be at peace."

I suggested to her that if she had shopping to do, she do it. She could stay in the nurses' residence for two or three days. I did not hear from her until she arrived in her home. The letter was full of gratitude. The sweetness and love in her letter I have never forgotten. She invited me come and spend my vacation with her family and to come soon. Before we went to the hospital, she said, "What will I tell my family?" I said: "Tell them you did not pass the physical examination. You would like to stay in Denver for a few months for the experience before coming home."

One morning one of the professors of the medical school came into my office to ask a favor of me. His very close friend in the East had written him that his daughter had been dismissed from one of the large nursing schools and the reason why. He asked if I would consider admitting her to our school. I said: "You know me well enough to know I am a disciplinarian, but a humanitarian as well. I admit her with the next class because they are your friends, because you ask it, and because I have faith in youth."

She came, a very bright, attractive young woman. I brought her into the office to get acquainted, told her what we expected from our students and what she could expect of us. We would put up with no nonsense. She made good, graduated, and returned to her home and married.

I saw her in the East, and she told me she had married an alcoholic. Billy Sunday had been in the East, and her husband suggested that they attend his meeting. After the first one, he asked to attend all. He was absolutely cured. They moved to a large ranch and were active and busy church workers. I receive Christmas greetings every Christmas. Recently when I came west, she called to tell me of her family, three boys and a girl, and how happy they were. Her gratitude was deep indeed, and she promised they would see me soon. The gratitude of the family was deep.

The doors to the nursing offices were never closed; the door to my own office was never closed. There was never a problem too small or too great for me to listen to. When there were complaints involving two or more persons, I would suggest they get together or bring them together in my office and in this way solve them. There is no problem which cannot be solved through understanding, sitting down and discussing it; and we really had no problems in the school. We practiced the Golden Rule and it was carried out.

In 1930 the Rockefeller Foundation offered a three-month fellowship to deans and directors of university schools at Yale University. University schools of nursing were still in their infancy. The fellowship was for meeting deans and directors, setting standards, and stabilizing and unifying university schools of nursing. It was very helpful in every way.

On my return I was received by the educational director with "Oh, I am glad you are back." I asked her what happened.

She replied: "Miss ——— (a student) is pregnant and about to deliver. I don't know what to do."

I answered, "Will you ask her to come to my office." She was in the operating room, wore the operating gowns, and her pregnancy was not too noticeable. She was a beautiful young woman, a daughter of one of the old and proud families.

I asked her if she was pregnant. She said "Yes." I asked her if she was in love with the young man. She answered they had been in love for several years. Her family would not hear of her getting married. I asked her no personal questions but said I would have to tell her mother.

She said, "Oh, no!"

I said, "I will go to your home immediately after this conference and bring her back with me."

She said, "You will not leave me alone with her, will you?"

I said, "There is no reason to, unless you or she wish it."

She returned to the operating room.

I went to see her mother. She received me graciously. I said: "I have come to talk with you about your daughter. I have just returned after three months' absence and found her pregnant and about ready to deliver." She got out of her chair and with all her dignity said, "Miss Kieninger, you cannot come to this house and say that about our daughter."

Then I asked her if she would come with me and see for herself. She came. She met the daughter. It was a sad meeting. I then said, "I can and will take care of her if you wish me to."

I called the Salvation Army Hospital and asked if they could take care of a friend of mine. They replied they could, and I said we would send the patient right out. I asked the mother if she would take her. "I will arrange for the service and have the marriage certificate dated back one year. I will call the bishop and ask him to send out one of his assistants." I asked the mother if she would give her consent to the marriage.

She said "Yes."

"Will tomorrow at eight o'clock be all right for the marriage?"

She said "Yes."

The mother and the young man were there when the priest and I arrived. The intern was also there. I had forgotten about the ring and asked the mother if she would let them use her ring. She did. Immediately after the service, she was placed on the table and delivered of a seven-pound girl. The intern brought the child to our baby ward. The child was adopted in about two weeks by a close friend of mine. She is happily married and has a lovely family of several children.

I suggested she stay out of school for the rest of the year and enter the following fall class. This she did. She asked me once if I would tell her where the baby was. I told her she had been adopted out of the city by a lovely family and I could not tell her. (That was a very hard thing for me to say.)

Capping was always a happy event: the cap, the symbol of honor; the Florence Nightingale lamp, the symbol of consecration and dedication; the uniform, the symbol of service.

We had chapel meeting in the morning led by the students. These were short—perhaps only a prayer, perhaps only a psalm, and perhaps only some music and a song or poem—but we came together, the faculty and the students, and thus started the day with kind thoughts. If a student had a suggestion or an idea, she could bring it up at that time.

There was student government and the students governed well. Many of the university affairs were attended by the students. The big problem was, of course, transportation. Two rules were always observed: the uniform was not to be worn on the street, and the cap was not to be worn off duty.

In the final graduation at the university, the students chose to wear their white uniforms and their capes, which were the colors of the university, a lovely bluish gray with gold lining. They preferred these to the black gowns and mortarboards worn by the students and faculty of the university.

Time marched on, and the three months had slid into fifteen years. It was really time for that nurse with the master's degree to take on the school.

Our nursing faculty was active in local, state, and national nursing offices. I had been active also in local professional and civic affairs.

One of my close friends, the traveling executive secretary of the National Education Association, stopped often in Denver on her travels west. On one occasion she mentioned that the national headquarters were planning the International Conference in Denver in the summer. I asked her if she would like me to give a tea for them. She was delighted. When I mentioned the tea to a close friend in Denver, she said, "Let me give it for you." I was delighted. Her beautiful home and garden would be a perfect setting. She said her daughter was a member of the Junior League, and she and her friends would be happy to serve or do whatever there was to do. It was a pleasure to meet so many foreign educators. The service of the beautiful young girls added much with their charm and grace. There were between three and four hundred guests. I was indeed grateful for my gracious friends.

It was 1941 and war seemed imminent. I was asked to come to our national headquarters and assist in setting up the nursing program for defense nursing, which later, when war was declared, became the National Council of Nursing for War Service.

I resigned to report to headquarters. The American Red Cross in Denver presented me with a large, beautiful silk Red Cross flag and a large, beautiful American flag. I had also received a Lamp of Service from the American Nurses Association. My faithful, loyal co-worker and friend, Miss Colestock, asked me to leave these for the school. I was happy to do so and leave them to the school that had given me so much joy, such pleasure, so much harmony, and friendships that have endured to this day. I missed beautiful Colorado and its glorious mountains, its waterfalls, its climate. I would miss my fine, loyal, and faithful staff. Once again I was starting on a new project. The door had been opened.

CHAPTER 9

Wartime Service and Back to Brazil

The plan for defense nursing was just being set up. The national executive secretary had her desk in a very small office of the National Nursing Association office in New York, and I had my desk with all the secretaries. I immediately employed a secretary for myself. We carried on for a few weeks until we could find larger quarters. Fortunately there were offices in the same building which lent themselves very well to our needs.

About this time Brazil had broken diplomatic relations with Germany, and war was imminent. Brazil asked for help in setting up their emergency nursing and first-aid program, and I was given a leave of absence for six months to return to Brazil. I stayed eighteen months. There was a need not only for war service but also for checking schools of nursing in South America and helping generally with nursing.

I was flown to Brazil in an army plane with three very high-ranking officers. We traveled only by daylight. It took three days to make the journey. When we arrived in Rio, I came to the door of the plane and saw three photographers. I stepped back into the plane. I was sure they were there for the officers. The photographers, however, asked that I come out, as they were looking for me. They took photographs. I had had a great deal of publicity in Brazil, but it was all a surprise to me.

It was a short walk from the plane to the door of the airport, and as we approached the door I heard singing. I recognized the school song. When I entered the door, there was the entire student body and the graduates of the school—all in student nurses' uniforms. When I stepped up to greet them, they pelted me with rose petals carried in their aprons. The graduates wore the student uniforms to carry the petals in their aprons and also to make me feel at home. I knew then that Brazil had not forgotten me, and certainly I had not forgotten Brazil.

That was the beginning of almost eighteen most interesting months. The emergency program was begun and carried on under our supervision and our efficient graduates. I gave most of my attention to schools, consultation, the setting-up of shorter emergency nursing courses in the interior, and helping where I was needed.

My arrival in Brazil in 1921 had occurred during the world's fair in Rio. One of the sister nations in South America had presented Brazil with a beautiful hotel. It was located at the entrance of beautiful Guanabara Bay under Corcovado Mountain, on which is a magnificent statue of Christ, "Christ of Corcovado." The hotel was accepted but never used at all, as it was too far from the fairgrounds and presented transportation problems. Several years after I left in 1926, the school had outgrown its second home, and the government turned the hotel over to the school for its home.

It is a palatial building and lends itself beautifully for a nurses' residence. It has a really beautiful entrance hall with marble stairs leading to the second hall. On the first floor is a huge dining room and a huge lounge and guest rooms. The home was beautifully furnished. On the second floor is another large lounge, and there are two smaller connecting rooms which were to have been used for the bar. These were turned into chapels. One had a magnificent statue of Mother Mary on the altar, and it was much used every day. The second one, the connecting room, had a magnificent statue of beloved Jesus. There were no seats in this room, just a prayer bench.

The International Nurses Convention was to be held in Chile in December of 1942, the heart of the summer. I wanted Dona Lais, the director of the school, to go, but she felt she could not at this particular time. We selected two of the outstanding graduates to represent the school, and I suggested that she also send two seniors. We got them ready and sent them on their way. I had not planned to attend. I do not speak Spanish, and we had excellent representatives.

The day before the opening of the convention, I received, through the Rockefeller International Health Board, a cablegram from the American Nurses Association asking me to represent them, which includes the American Nurses Association, the Public Health Nurses Association, the Collegiate School of Nurses Association, the Private Duty Nurses Association, and the American Red Cross. There was only one flight a day, and the plane had already left. The next morning I was on my way, the day of the opening of the convention. I would arrive for the opening meeting that evening.

We changed planes on the top of the Andes Mountains on the boundary line between Peru and Chile, not too far from their magnificent statue of the Christ of the Andes, made of the weapons intended for war melted down to make this most significant memorial to peace. On the base are carved these words: "These mountains will crumble to dust ere Peru and Chile break the peace which at the feet of the Christ the Redeemer they have sworn to keep."

I arrived in Santiago at 5:00 p.m. and went to the hotel. At 6:00 p.m. came a delegation of nurses to welcome me, among them our own delegates, for which I was grateful. The delegation was very enthusiastic and happy and told me of the happenings during the day. When they got up to leave, they said: "Senhora, dinner will be at eight. You are the honored guest and the main speaker of the meeting tonight."

It was a little shock, but there was no point in remonstrating. I said, "I must have some interpreters, since I do not speak Spanish, nor do I remember Portuguese well enough to give a speech." They said they could furnish all the interpreters I needed. I asked our beloved delegate to do the interpreting for me into Portuguese; but I also had to be interpreted into Spanish, and she did not speak Spanish. I told them I could help them in their conferences and discussions, but to have to speak and be interpreted through two persons would be beyond all expectations.

They said not to worry; they would find someone and they would pick me up about seven forty-five. They found someone who could speak English, Spanish and Portuguese. I then asked them, would they please leave so I could get my thoughts together? Fortunately I had unpacked my bag before they came. I knew there was nothing I could do but go through with it. They were a happy group. There were many distinguished guests present at the banquet, and apparently well pleased with what the interpreter told them.

The entire convention was a happy affair. There were many social activities, and they had made appointments for me with dignitaries. "You must meet them and they must meet you," they said.

Before I left New York for Brazil, I had attended a convention of our own national organizations. The difference between the dignified, serious-minded leaders of home and these gay and happy ones was quite a contrast. I thoroughly enjoyed the convention and the gaiety, and yet they were serious too. They made some excellent resolutions and plans. I hoped the resolutions would be fulfilled. The report of the convention was written up, as were all my appointments, and all put in a lovely book by one of the delegates and presented for me, for which I was grateful. I was happy to send it to the American Nurses Association. It was a joy to meet and be one of them for a few days. Every moment of the day was taken with appointments and luncheons and, of course, meetings.

Christmas was almost upon us. I left Santiago the morning of the twenty-fourth for Rio. We changed planes where we changed before, on the boundary line between Peru and Chile. It was a magnificent experience; the Christ of the Andes seemed very close. The feeling of His power and presence was tremendous. There were two American engineers on the plane. They were professors of the University of Colorado I had known in Colorado, and they were on a government mission. It was a joy to see them.

Upon Arrival in Rio

I arrived in Rio about eight o'clock and arrived home about eight-thirty. I found a busy Dona Lais (the director) and students preparing for the Christmas celebration at midnight. Christmas is a holy and most sacred day in South America. Again, the Christ child in the crèche was beautifully and magnificently dressed. I wrapped packages for Dona Lais while they finished preparations for the midnight service. I was so grateful to be a part of that glorious Christmas celebration. At 5:00 a.m. was the Christmas mass.

Brazil

As usual, when I arrived home, my room was full of beautiful flowers with an abundance of my favorite orchids. I did not go with Dona Lais to her brother's family for Christmas Day. Her brother had recently passed away. I felt it was a family day. In fact, I did not go out at all, but enjoyed a beautiful day. Our suites on the second floor opened with long French doors on the balcony and on "Christ of Corcovado." It was a day of peace and quiet. Dona Lais came home early and we sat together on the balcony in the peace and radiance of the Christ Child emanating His love to encircle the entire globe.

Dona Lais asked me to help her set up an emergency nursing program in Victoria in the interior. I was happy to do it. Our American engineers were supervising a sanitary program and the building of roads, water, and light in the interior. They had their headquarters in Victoria.

In a few days we were on our way. It was a day's journey to Victoria. The cook packed a large basket of food, enough for a family. Everyone on the train had baskets of food, and most of them were eating all the time. We had three meals on the train. It was really fun. Pigs squealing, chickens cackling, roosters crowing—it was interesting to see the natives. They had been in

Rio and were bringing home their wares. They were happy and seemed to be enjoying their food and each other.

The train looked like a toy. The engine was small, the tracks narrow-gauge, the car open. The scenery was beautiful. Several times during the journey the little engine ran off the tracks, and the men on the train put it back. Even though the day seemed long, the benches hard and uncomfortable, we had a fun-filled day. Everybody was eating; it was simply a continuous meal. We finally arrived at our destination. There had been a place prepared for us to stay.

The next morning we called on the priest of the parish to pay our respects—a practice I had established twenty years before—and tell him the reason and purpose for being there. On our way to see him, we passed a very large beautiful vacant house on a big plot of ground. It seemed to be what we would need, although we had not seen the inside of it. We called on the mayor, or the *prefeito,* of the village and asked him about the house and told him why we were interested. He told us about the owner and said, "He will never, never let you have it." We did not go to see the owner, but did go back to the priest and told him we needed that particular house. It would answer our purposes perfectly. He said, "Be at peace."

Shortly thereafter came word that the beautiful home was available for our service. The house served our needs perfectly. There were three very large rooms on the first floor. One was arranged as a classroom, one as a dining room, and the third as a dormitory. We made double bedrooms of the bedrooms already there; I took the smallest room for myself. We also used the classroom for a chapel.

The bathroom was a real joy—very large and equipped with one needle shower and spray, two large tubs, and a sitz bath. We divided it with curtains. Several persons could take baths at the same time in privacy. Dona Lais felt she must return to Rio.

I asked her to send three well-prepared graduates, all with teaching ability—one with public health experience, one with executive ability who would take on the project at my departure. In the meantime I had interviewed young women for the course. Dona Lais and I had planned a very simple uniform. Those who were accepted made them. We accepted twelve.

One afternoon I was sitting on the steps of the front porch for

Guanabara Bay,
Rio de Janeiro, 1943

a breath of air. Suddenly there appeared a large army of ants, huge and black. They made for the rosebushes in full bloom. In less time than it takes to write this, they stripped the bush of roses and leaves and disappeared. Where they came from and where they went I do not know. It made me heartsick.

I called on the priest to tell him of our progress. Students would be admitted in a few days. The graduates from Rio would be there the next day. I asked him if he would come to give the house a blessing as well as the students and personnel. He said he would be happy to do so.

The priest had recommended the cook, a maid and houseman. The house was in excellent condition. The students had invited their families and a very few friends. The graduates arrived. The students were admitted, and the priest gave a blessing to the home and the rooms and personnel. There was the usual coffee after the dedication service.

The next morning classes began. The graduates from Rio had brought the necessary books and equipment. I opened the school by explaining the ideal of nursing and the rules and regulations which we had established in the home and school. Brazilian young women are very dedicated and very consecrated. It was a joy to see their devotion, as they say, "to God and our country."

Often on Sundays the American engineers would come to Victoria for dinner at noon or early lunch before returning. The cook was fond of them, and there was nothing too good or too much trouble to feed them well and send them back Sunday evenings with a basket of food and delicacies. They were a group of fine men, and we thoroughly enjoyed them. They were fun, too. It was a break for them to come, and it was lovely to have them.

There were twelve students; all completed their course and were started on public health nursing under the supervision of our public health nurses. They did not wear nursing caps, but arm bands with the initials "V.S.P." (Visitadores de Saúde Pública).

I returned to Rio after the ceremony. There was always much to do in Rio: conferences, visits, plans. Some of the students who completed their emergency course in Victoria were later admitted into the Anna Nery School in Rio and graduated from there. The course set up for emergency nursing and first aid (lay group) in Rio was progressing very well.

Before the first soldiers were sent into combat, a mass was given for them with communion service. The mass was held in the Jardim República, the large and very beautiful garden in Rio. Nelson Rockefeller was in Rio at the time, and he was invited to sit with other dignitaries in the box of the bishop. Dona Lais and I were also invited in the bishop's box. It was a most solemn occasion, about seven hundred soldiers. After it was over and I expressed my gratitude to the bishop, he extended his hand and in his holy and gracious manner replied: "I remember you well. You brought the first nurses of Brazil to the cathedral for the blessing of their caps twenty years ago."

Mr. Rockefeller made a good impression in Brazil and was well liked. He was royally entertained, professionally and socially, among the Brazilians especially. He decided to give an informal buffet for the Brazilians, and I was invited. I felt I should go early. When I arrived, some of the guests were already there and enjoying the buffet, but he was not there. He had been delayed.

I received his guests for him. It was an enjoyable occasion.

In 1963 when The Summit Lighthouse published its *Encyclical* by the great master El Morya, I sent Mr. Rockefeller a copy. His reply was "we are on our way to Europe, but I will take it with me and read it on the trip." I think it was his wedding trip. I prayed he might study it and use it.

Dona Lais with Clara Louise in her room, 1943

Time was marching on, and it was again time for my departure. The graduation certificates had been given in an impressive ceremony for those (the lay group) who took the emergency war course of nursing and first aid. I had been away from New York for almost eighteen months and felt I must get back. Before I left, I asked Dona Lais what I could do to repay the Brazilians for their love and their grace and all they had done for me. She said, "Would you like to educate a priest?" I said I would love to. Arrangements were made for me to do so. I did not meet the young man, but the gratitude of the church was deeply expressed in the personal calls of many members of the church.

In a letter I received from the hierarchy of the Catholic church before my departure, the opening words were "Even though you are not a Catholic, your love and devotion to Brazil, her welfare, and her people have endeared you to our hearts. We ask you to remain with us and make Brazil your home. We need you. You have done much for our youth, and people. We need you and Brazil needs you...." I placed that letter in the history of

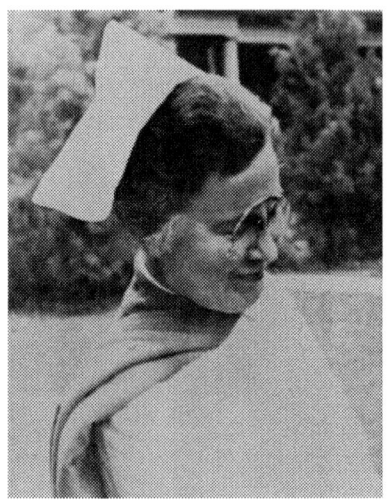

The Joy of Pinning
Escola de Enfermeiras D. Anna Nery, Rio de Janeiro

their school, which I sent them some years ago.

This time I traveled by plane. My rooms were again filled with gifts, flowers, and a beautiful corsage of three very large magnificent orchids for me to wear. There were many telegrams. It was difficult to say goodbye. I asked Dona Lais that she and the graduates and students not come to the airport. Before leaving Brazil, I flew to Victoria to inspect the stability of the nursing program we had set up. We flew over a small, crystal-clear lake through a double rainbow, and I felt it was the great amen to the work I had done in South America.

In 1963 I sent a history of the Anna Nery School, mostly pictures taken from the opening days of the school until I left. The pictures were of the progress, professional and social events.

Because Mother Mary is the adored Mother of every home in South America and her picture or statue adorns every home, because São Francesco de Assisi is the patron of the Hospital São Francesco de Assis in which the medical and nursing students received their practical training, because South America is the land of immortal promise in its domain in the future of mankind and the Great Divine Director is the Manu of that future race, I asked these magnificent cosmic beings if they would send a blessing for South America that might be placed in my book for them as a blessing to everyone who reads it and a focus for their activity. This was graciously and lovingly done through our messenger.

Chapter 10

New York

The door had never been closed to my position in New York with the nursing council; it was still open even though it had been temporarily filled. I was gone almost eighteen months instead of six. When I phoned the executive secretary of my return, she said, "Come right along; we are waiting for you." That was in 1943. My title was Associate Executive Director in Charge of Administration. The executive director was in charge of the program. I remained three months after peace was restored to the world in 1945 to help with the history and closing of that particular activity. It was a tremendous program; the history of it is in the libraries and archives of the nursing association. It was an accelerated program to prepare more nurses for war service and to increase admissions to the nursing schools.

When I had left the council to go to Brazil, it was just being organized and they were moving into new quarters. When I returned I found it had expanded to two floors. I was delighted to be with the busy group again and stay put for the duration. I seemed to be the general manager doing what I could to keep a complex and busy organization harmonious and running smoothly. When I returned I found the secretarial staff smoking at their work. I said nothing to them, but followed my custom. I called a conference of the secretaries, did not mention their smoking, but asked if they had anything to bring up or any suggestions or questions. I then asked them if they would like a coffee break, fifteen minutes in the morning and fifteen minutes in the afternoon. Then they could enjoy their cigarettes and coffee in peace. They could have it in the rest room or they could go to the drugstore. Our office was on Seventh and Broadway, and there were many drugstores and coffee shops around. They were delighted and the smoking stopped.

But there was one problem, that of time. We had a number of Jewish secretaries and clerks on the staff whose holidays did not coincide with Gentile holidays. They would always be off duty on their holidays, and they had more holidays than the Gentiles did, thus getting more off time. The other secretaries felt that it was not fair. I suggested that we add the extra days that the Jewish employees had for their holidays to the Gentiles' vacations. That settled that problem and made them happy.

The secretaries had established the practice of serving tea in the afternoon to the executives. The secretaries took turns putting on the water, the cups, cookies, or whatever there was. When the water was hot, each secretary would serve her executive. It took very little time, and everyone enjoyed it. I had a Jewish friend in the West who almost always kept us supplied with cakes, cookies and delicacies, for which Jewish cooking is famous. We had a very harmonious group, and everyone seemed happy.

The offices had to be covered six days a week. The secretarial staff worked only five. Since I had no home or family, I volunteered to cover the office on Saturday and did so. Occasionally one of the executive secretaries would come in.

One day on our way to lunch, I noticed a young woman coming down the walk dressed in a pink suit and wearing a large hat. I paid special attention to her because of the pink suit and her large hat. When she stepped off the sidewalk onto the street, I recognized her. She also recognized me and burst into tears.

She was a brilliant young woman and a friend from Brazil. She had come from Rio to Washington and New York to do some research work and was looking for me, she said. She did not know in which hotel I would be. We stopped the traffic on Seventh and Broadway while she wept, first because of her loneliness and disappointment and then in gratitude. I told her we would meet that night at dinner and in the meantime I would see what I could do to help her. She knew no one and asked if I had someone with whom she could stay while she was doing her research in Washington.

I told her that I had two friends in Washington whom I would call. One was the field secretary for the National Education Association, but she would be in the field most of the time. The other was a playmate of mine who was married, had two children, both in the service. I phoned the latter first and the husband answered. I told him my story and asked if they would be willing to take her into their home for a short period of time. I knew her well; she was from one of Brazil's finest families, and there would be no trouble. He replied that Elise, his wife, was in the hospital recuperating from an operation. He would call her and then call me back.

In a short time he phoned and said they had decided that since she was a friend of mine, they would gladly share their home with her. Their daughter-in-law also made her home with them. We met at dinner that night, and I was so happy to tell her the good news. She left the next day for Washington, remaining six months. It was a most happy arrangement for all. They formed a lasting friendship. The gratitude of Dona Ignace is still expressing itself in gifts and letters to them. It was and is a most happy and joyous relationship.

One of the services I rendered, by choice, was to help our out-of-town board members and other professional persons to find hotel accommodations. It was almost impossible to find even a room of any kind, especially on Saturdays. There just were none. I contacted Mr. Smith, one of the managers of the Hotel Pennsylvania, explained to him the importance of our service and the many calls we had for hotel rooms. He explained his problems to me, which of course I knew, but said he would do what he could, although he would not always be able to accommodate us. We established a fine business relationship, and he was really a friend in need. Most of the time he found rooms.

One Saturday morning at six o'clock, my sister called me from North Carolina and said her son Charles and five other boys were on their way to New York for the weekend. Would I find rooms for them or a place for them to stay? They were young musicians and wanted to hear their favorite orchestra leader, who was very popular at that time. They were on their way. There was nothing to say with six boys descending on me on a Saturday, eighteen or nineteen years of age. She said they would be there in a couple of hours. She had given Charles my telephone number and he would call me.

At eight o'clock I phoned Mr. Smith, my friend at the Pennsylvania Hotel, and told him I was in a peck of trouble, more trouble than he had! He said, "I am in a bushel of trouble." I told him there were six boys coming up for the weekend, and he said there was not a room available anyplace. I said: "What shall I do with them? I can't hang them on a pole or let them run the streets." I said, "I'm to meet them in the lobby of your hotel; then I'll come and talk with you and we'll see what we can do for them."

When my nephew called a little later, I told him I would meet them at the Hotel Pennsylvania, which was across the street from Penn Station. Truly, great is the love and power of God! When I arrived I saw five frightened boys standing near the door. As I stepped up to them, they all spoke at once: "Are you Aunt Louise?" I said, "Yes, I am she. Where is Charles?" "He is looking for you."

Soon he appeared and I took him to Mr. Smith, who talked to him and told him he had no place for them. But he was studying him all the time. Finally he said to me, "The only place I have in this hotel is the bridal suite." I thought, can I imagine six young boys in that gorgeous bridal suite? Then Mr. Smith said to Charles, "Simpson, I'm going to give you the bridal suite. I am doing it for your aunt, and I trust you absolutely to take care of it." I said to Charles, "I know you, Charles, but I do not know your companions." He assured me that we could trust them, that they were from good homes and the families were friends.

I told Mr. Smith he need not worry, that I would be responsible for the six. I went with them to the suite—two very large, gorgeously furnished rooms, a living room and a bedroom with twin beds. Mr. Smith, thoughtful as he was, ordered four extra cots put in so the six could be together. We had a little conference. I asked the boys, "How many smoke?" I knew Charles did not, but the others must have been too frightened to say whether they did or not. I said: "Just in case you take a notion to smoke, Charles, will you now order five more ashtrays, one for each of you. When you smoke, carry the ashtrays around with you and clean them after you use them. Hang up your towels, straighten up your beds, and keep the rooms in perfect order; but enjoy them and have fun."

I then left them. We were to meet that evening at the Hotel Commodore, where their hero was playing. Charles was so engrossed with him and the music he almost forgot to eat. After dinner they asked to entertain me, but I left them to enjoy Broadway or whatever else they wished to do. They offered to attend church with me the next morning, but I refused and invited them to dinner with me on Sunday night at a Swedish smorgasbord. They really enjoyed the food; there was no orchestra to distract them. They then took me to the bus and went their way to enjoy the evening as they wished. I bade them goodbye. They left for home on Monday morning.

On Monday I called Mr. Smith at the hotel and he said to me, "*What* did you do to those boys?" I asked, "Why?" And he said: "They left the suite in perfect order; one would hardly know anyone had been in it. They can come again any time." Busy as he was, Mr. Smith was always courteous and could usually find accommodations that I asked for, but not always. I was grateful for a friend such as he proved to be.

During this time I had been invited by Mrs. Roosevelt to a meeting at the White House. She had invited the women of various business and professional organizations for a conference on how women may share in a postwar policy-making. I attended the first one; we met each other and they were a most interesting group. She then asked us if we would come early at 9:00 a.m. the next morning prepared to spend the day and night in the White House.

I had been her dinner guest in her apartment in New York and met her on several occasions. Before leaving, I asked her if it would be all right with her if I asked the president of the American Nurses Association to take my place on the committee. She would be president for several years longer. I was retiring and I had been out of the country, and the president could serve much better than I. She accepted her, but she said, "You come too." She was a most gracious, friendly, and courteous person, interested in everything, a tireless worker. I did not go back.

There was perfect harmony and cooperation in our organization. I remember one evening, just as the secretaries were going out of the door, a call came from Washington to send out a thousand telegrams. The secretaries had remained to see what the telephone call was about. Every one of them remained. We had the schools and heads listed by the state, and it really was not a great chore. We sent a list by the state and a copy of the night letter to the Western Union, and they did the rest. Orders like that were not unusual, but that was the only order for a thousand.

The war was coming to an end. We had furnished the office with used furniture, and we were planning to sell it. I called the secretaries together and asked if each secretary would like to clean their own typewriter, polish her desk, chair and table, as we planned to sell it and could get much more for it if it looked good after several years of hard wear. They thought it was a good idea and did so. The furniture, polished as it was, brought a great deal more money after several years of hard wear than when we had bought it in the beginning.

We said goodbye to the faithful, loyal, and cooperative staff, to whom nothing was ever too much or too little to do. The reports were written; the files and records were placed in the archives of the American Nurses Association; and the National Nursing Council for Defense, later for War Service, became history, adding another grand chapter in the record of women's contribution to the nation's glory.

Some of our secretaries were offered positions with the American Nurses Association, but none accepted. There was no Social Security there at that time. Some of them we never saw again; others remained friends, especially the executives. I really had no thought of tomorrow, knowing that the hand of God, who opened every door for me on the path, would open another in which I could be of service to Him, the Great Host of Heaven, and to our country. I was asked to join the staff of the American Nurses Association, but I refused the offer.

Chapter 11

Service to the Masters

I had met the beautiful leader of the I AM activity in New York in her gracious sanctuary. Mrs. Mary Myneta Boos had invited me on several occasions to spend the weekend with her in her Scarsdale home during the war. I had not accepted; there was not time, as every moment of my time was taken up—six days a week work and Sunday to rest and do the things I needed to do personally. I had attended the sanctuary when I could, however.

After the war was over, I did accept her gracious invitation and spent two weeks with her and her family at her beautiful country estate. This opened the door to a friendship that has lasted from that moment until now and always will. She and her husband offered me their home and asked me to stay and share it with them. I suggested we try it for a year. At the end of the year, if we were happy, I would stay. I did. I enjoyed them and their family, saw their children grow up, and formed a friendship that will last throughout all eternity.

In the spring of 1948 or '49, Mrs. Ballard invited Mrs. Boos and me to be her guests in the masters' home in Denver on the way to the masters' retreat in the Rocky Mountains. This had been a lodge and overlooked the beautiful Ouray valley surrounded by towering peaks. Entering the door into this fragrant and peaceful retreat, one truly left the busy world. The large lounge with its huge fireplace was quiet and peaceful for study and meditation. One felt the peace of the mountains. The large glassed and screened porch was used for meals and conferences. Truly one felt the reverence, love, and quiet of the masters and the great mountains.

In discussing activities with Mrs. Ballard, she told of her desire and plan to organize a youth headquarters. They had purchased property in Mount Shasta, California, the summer-school campus and buildings of the University of California, also the high school building of Mount Shasta. She discussed her plans and asked if I would be interested in organizing it. Since most of my years had been spent with youth, I said I would be happy to try it.

In a few days we motored to Mount Shasta. The trip was delightful. We motored to the campus, a jewel at the foot of the majestic Mount Shasta. We arrived at the little village of Mount Shasta in the late afternoon. I was delighted at the layout. It seemed to be exactly what we were looking for and to answer our purpose, which it really did.

We returned to the village several blocks from the campus and inspected the high school. It, too, would answer the purpose for which we wanted it with little alteration. I remember two apple trees in the yard, not too healthy but bearing apples. Mrs. Ballard blessed them and said that the next year they would produce a good crop. They did.

Soon Mrs. Ballard and Mrs. Boos returned to Colorado. Mrs. Ballard left but one request, that I secure the flour the Mormons use, and said I could get it from the Mormons. She did not say what Mormons or where they were, but I wrote until I found them. I told her I would phone her every evening and report our progress.

The high school had been the property of Mr. and Mrs. McCorkle. He was a retired construction engineer, she a teacher of music. Her plan was to start a school of music. There were five in the family—a bachelor son, a widowed daughter, and a beautiful young granddaughter about seven. They certainly were real ascended master friends. There was nothing they couldn't do and didn't do and weren't happy to do. I had dinner with them that night. We made reservations for me at the little hotel about fifteen miles away. I would breakfast at the hotel. Noonday and evening meals were with them. Bob, the son, would chauffeur me back and forth until we could make other arrangements.

Mount Shasta was a village of about three hundred, a post office, a few shops, and a courthouse. The villagers were not too happy to have us, but that was overcome in time. The McCorkles remained in the home for the three years that I was there and were a great help in every way. They lived in the school building, using the back part of the school. Mrs. McCorkle was a very fine musician. They used the large assembly room as their family room. On the large platform she placed her grand piano and organ. Every morning at six o'clock, for one hour she sent her beautiful music into the spheres.

There was much to be done, and the time was short before the guests would be arriving. The campus was to be made ready, cleaned, painted if necessary; and accommodations had to be found for the students. A place had to be found to buy food, and headquarters had to be made ready. I called Mrs. Ballard every evening after dinner to report our progress. In this way we kept in touch. It was a great satisfaction to me and to her. Time was marching on fast.

One evening after I had called her (the only public phone was on the little main street), I stood on the curb and really wondered how I would find enough food for hundreds of people. There were to be two groups each two weeks, the young people the first two weeks and the older persons the third and fourth weeks. There probably would be from three to four hundred people, perhaps more. Standing there thinking about it, I did not worry; for I knew that God who had opened all doors on my path would open that one too.

Down the street came a truck. I noticed the name "The California Food and Produce Company." I motioned him to stop. He came over to see what I wanted. I told him a little about our project and the probable number of people we would have to feed. He said his company served the surrounding towns and villages and would be able to take care of us, that he made three trips a week to Mount Shasta. I asked him to stop at headquarters the following Monday, which would be on his next trip. We established a fine business relationship. He was truly another friend in need. The company was in Yreka, fifteen miles away.

On my first Sunday, as I sat in the office of headquarters looking over the mail, someone knocked at the door. In came a young man, an accountant, with his equipment and supplies, ready for business. I was indeed grateful to see him. We quickly arranged a room for him with Mrs. McCorkle and also arranged for him to have a private office. He came in his car, which we needed.

I did not have to worry about personnel; Mrs. Ballard took care of that. Reporting to her as I did every night was very helpful, as it kept her in touch with our progress and needs, and in a few days the required personnel would be there. The baker, the cook, and those in charge of the various activities came out a few days before the campus opened, as did some of the others who were to do certain services.

In surveying the high school building, we took over the front part with a small room at one side of the large hall, which was the sanctuary established by and for the one family of the activity who lived there. On the other side were large rooms with a bath. We used the large front room that opened off the hall for general business affairs of headquarters. We divided the second room into six cubicles—four for sleeping, a bathroom, and a supply room. I then lived there and had my meals with the McCorkles.

Then came the cleaning and preparation of the campus. There were a number of small cabins, one with two rooms and a bath. There was a large assembly room with a huge fireplace at one end and a huge stage at the other. There was a very large dining room, a good-sized kitchen, and a bakery shop. That was one unit. There were also the bathrooms and laundry and the cellar underground.

They were in fairly good repair, but all had to be cleaned. The kitchen had to have some repairs on the stove, and the bathrooms needed plumbing and painting. Where it was necessary, we painted; but there were very few rooms where it was necessary. Windows, floors, and woodwork had to be cleaned. The little suite with the bathroom, we prepared for Mrs. Ballard. Knowing her favorite color was pink, we did everything in pink. She did not sleep there, but used it during the day for conferences and appointments. We prepared a first-aid section behind the huge curtains of the assembly hall stage, but it was never needed. In it we placed two cots for those who might wish to rest.

The McCorkles were the greatest help. The second and third young men had arrived, and then the fourth. We were very busy, but it was really fun. Miracles were really accomplished. Mrs. McCorkle was a beautiful musician, and often I would ask her to play for me. She did with all the love of her beautiful talent.

The biggest problem was to find sleeping rooms and accommodations for our guests. There were no motels anywhere. There was nothing in Mount Shasta. The nearest hotel was fifteen miles away and accommodated about thirty persons. We engaged that immediately for sleeping and placed our staff there. The next one was about twenty-five miles away. We engaged all the rooms the hotel could spare. They had to reserve some for travelers. Then we canvassed homes. In time we found sufficient beds in houses within a radius of ten to fifteen miles. There were no single beds anywhere; double beds had to be used. We tried to put those who came from the same cities together. There was no time to advise the students of the double beds. They said not one word about the double beds. They were a group of wonderful young men and women.

Then there was the transportation problem. We hired the two school buses. These started service at six o'clock in the morning to bring the personnel first and then students. We always had a huge fire in the fireplace in the large assembly hall when they arrived and hot drinks and food—usually sweet rolls, cakes, doughnuts, pie if they wanted it, and they always did. The baker and the kitchen personnel were on duty by 6:00 a.m. Breakfast was served at nine. We had excellent food. I was always up to greet and serve the students on their arrival in the morning.

I then conceived the idea of a beauty shop. There was a small beauty shop in the village, but it never could have taken care of our group. I called a friend in San Francisco and asked her if she knew of anyone or had a friend who was a beauty operator who would be willing to bring the necessary equipment and set up a shop for the conclave. She would be our guest. Shortly my friend phoned. She had contacted a friend who would be willing and delighted to come. We charged a small sum for beauty care, and the shop was a very popular place.

Mrs. Ballard sent the necessary personnel, and we were well covered in all departments. The first two weeks were for young students, the second two weeks for elderly students. It was a harmonious and delightful conference.

I asked Mrs. Ballard if she would appoint a youth as my assistant who could stay with us in Mount Shasta and be trained to take my place when I left. She was kind enough to ask me to select someone, which I did before the conference was over. I suggested to her also that at the next conference we invite the village fathers and their wives for a dinner at the end of the conference before we closed. We did invite them. Then I suggested that at the third conference we invite the business men, especially those who had been so helpful, and their wives. Long before this, however, headquarters had made friends with the village and its people. The youth made a most favorable impression on all they met.

The laundry room was a very pleasant room and lent itself well for the beauty shop and for washing and pressing dresses and small articles. We had an elderly student who did pressing and washing for the young people if they wished it. We decided to charge a small fee.

I made rounds to all the homes and rooms where our students were housed. Often after the evening service was over, one of the headquarters boys would take me on rounds, especially to the younger groups. They were well chaperoned. All seemed to be well.

The door to headquarters was never closed. I could not spend much time at headquarters with the conference several blocks away, but the door to my heart was always open. There was no formality about approaching me with anything anyone wished to know or anything I could do for anyone or any complaints or suggestions they might wish to make. The youth and I had several conferences and worked out a plan for expansion of their activities. There were no problems; they were always gracious and friendly, and they made an excellent impression on the village people. I was really proud of them. Everyone served with joy; everybody seemed to be happy. How could they help being so, under the radiance of the magnificent masters and the magnificent Mount Shasta?

After the second conference, the California Fruit and Produce Company asked if we would like some fruit which was not salable but was very good for canning. I accepted it with gratitude. The McCorkles and I canned three hundred jars and cans of preserves, jellies, and fruit for sauce (it was work but it was fun) for Mrs. Ballard to use as she wished to use it.

I remained for three years—three conferences. They were happy years of service. The assistant whom I chose and whom the leader appointed remained with us after the first conference, and under direction she conducted the second and third conferences without much help. She directed them with the joy and happiness of youth.

My service seemed to be finished, and the youth took over. I left soon for the East. The five permanent members of the staff gave a farewell dinner for me. A beautiful table with flowers, candles, and all that makes for joy. It was a joyous occasion, yet touched with sadness. I felt I would never attend another conference. When our business manager would settle for the dinner, the hotel manager said: "There is no bill. We will take no money for Miss Kieninger. She owns half of the hotel as it is and can have the rest of it if she asks for it."

When I said goodbye to them, they expressed their appreciation and admiration for the youth and all connected with the conference. The youth sent a beautiful letter of thanks. The part I loved most was the ending, "...but most of all we love you because you are you."

I soon left for New York. I never attended another conference and never saw Mount Shasta again, although the radiation and the radiance of that magnificent mountain had remained with me even now. I returned to New York, continued my home with the Boos family in Scarsdale, and assisted Mrs. Boos with her esoteric service in New York.

In the early spring of 1954, our beloved masters invited the student body to be the guests at the Royal Teton for two weeks, June 27 to July 11. On receipt of that invitation and instruction, I immediately wrote the chamber of commerce at the Royal

Teton for information regarding the names of the ranches and the home addresses of the owners. The resorts and ranches do not open for guests until late June. On receipt of the information, I wrote the homes of several ranch owners.

When that information came, we selected a large ranch right at the foot of the Grand Teton and reserved this for two weeks, June 27 to July 11. The first week, June 27 to July 4, was reserved for sanctuary and group leaders only; the second week, July 4 to 11, was for students also. There was no pioneering necessary. A few days before, Muriel Orr and I motored to the Grand Tetons to see if everything was in divine order and found it so. We had our morning and evening meals in the lodge dining room. Lunches were packed for those who wished them. The food was excellent.

The student body arrived on July 3. What a welcome we gave them. We had the entire park to ourselves. There was a small building with benches and an altar for prayer and meditation. To start out early in the morning and sing or yodel was a happy event; to go into the mountains or to walk to the little chapel at the entrance of the park or to sit quietly in the peace and radiation of the mountains was indescribable peace and almost lifted us into the mountain itself.

On July 10 we had a great picnic at Yellowstone Park. June 11 came all too soon. Reluctantly we turned our faces east with a heart full of gratitude to our magnificent masters. Which one of us can ever forget those blessed and happy days? They are eternal, and our gratitude is eternal for that great blessing.

Dress Uniform

CHAPTER 12

At the Summit of Life

In the evening of life when the sun rests sweetly and invitingly upon the mountains and the Light of God streams down in a mist of gold, my thoughts turn to the long ago when, as a young woman in immaculate white uniform and cap, the diploma of nursing in my hands, I stood before an open gate to a long path. The sun flashed its brilliant light through the branches of the trees, filling the pathway with blotches of gold; the field flowers sent their fragrance into the atmosphere. I stood there in deep gratitude and love to God and those who made it possible for me to fulfill my desire to become a nurse.

I had been consecrated and dedicated to service at my birth, at my confirmation, and again at our nurses' graduation. I had learned well the meaning of the Golden Rule as a child and what prayer and faith in God means. I made no plans. I knew there would be hills to climb, rivers to cross, days of sunshine and days of rain. I was unafraid. I will never forget our class motto, *Ich Dien*, nor the Golden Rule, which was taught us so well as children. *Ich dien* and the Golden Rule are a part of my life.

Soon I was offered a position as assistant to the director of a large nursing school, which I accepted but which was interrupted by the illness of our blessed mother. I made no plans. I never sought a position, either local or foreign. I never questioned the position offered. I felt the grace of God provided it, and I accepted it with gratitude to God. Even in foreign countries whose people I did not know, whose customs I did not know, I accepted, knowing the light of God never fails and that God's hand would lead me. I always had and always would to the end. When one door closed, another door opened.

I retired after World War II, remained in New York, and assisted the sanctuary leader with her esoteric program. During this time I spent three years in the West in an organization project. When that was accomplished, I returned to New York and continued to assist in the sanctuary.

In Atlantean days, within the compass of the city of New York was a great temple of Light. At the close of Atlantean culture the temples were destroyed, but the etheric temples remained. It was Mother Mary's desire to again establish a healing temple in this area. She sent an outline to be given in connection with the healing class on Tuesday evening. I was giving my own class every morning at five and asked if I might give Mother Mary's healing-class outline in the sanctuary every morning at six and open it to students. I was given permission. There were always students present. I was seldom alone. It was a happy class. When I resigned from the sanctuary, I continued with the class every morning and have continued. Where I go, the class is given and will be as long as I am in embodiment.

Time marches on. Years have passed quickly. I shared some of my early years with you, and I would like to share some of the activities of my later years.

The Summit Lighthouse

I have always been interested in esoteric teachings. Even in my young years I read and studied a great deal. Later I became very interested in several activities. Beautiful and spiritual they were. Unfortunately, the human crept in and I resigned. I was searching for a spiritual activity with a strong and selfless leadership—one who would put God and the Hierarchy of Heaven above all.

I was in Washington when The Summit Lighthouse was being organized. I met again the leader, Mark L. Prophet, whom I knew, and later his beautiful wife, Elizabeth. I attended the classes and met the students. There was harmony and peace. The magnificent instructions and dictations by the great ascended masters, their radiation and love, and the sincerity and simplicity of the messengers made me decide to remain longer. I felt I was finding what I had been searching for—strong leadership.

The messengers invited me to their home. I was delighted to see there a workshop—a busy staff of young men getting material ready to be sent to students and others. I voiced my joy and surprise. The messenger answered, "We live for the victory of the Light and to teach this knowledge to our students and mankind for their freedom and for the emancipation of our beloved America and our beloved planet." Knowing the messenger, his great love for God and the ascended hierarchy of heaven, for America and our beloved planet, his fearlessness and his experience, his integrity and his absolute honesty, his ability to meet any situation, business, governmental, and otherwise, I felt I had found what I had been looking for. He was well prepared to meet any situation, and there were many to meet I know.

The activity grew rapidly. I saw it grow from a handful of students to thousands in America and the world. There is discipline and understanding. The messengers not only share the ascended masters' dictations and teachings with the student body, but they keep students alert to world conditions and to what can be done through decrees to help mankind and the planet.

The messengers and their large staff are absolutely dedicated to selfless service to the ascended masters, America, and the world. At the quarterly conferences, students from all parts of

Elizabeth Clare Prophet and Mark L. Prophet

America and foreign countries meet each other and keep so busy there is not much time for visits. They are really magnificent meetings.

Now I would like to share with you excerpts from the ascended masters' letters. Saint Germain, the Knight Commander of the Keepers of the Flame Fraternity, wrote:

"Beloved friends of freedom, the requirements of the hour are constancy, harmony, and loyalty! For centuries men have tasted of the treasures of heaven; and for an equal time they have debated, delayed, and strained at the proper use of those same treasures. The heaven that might have manifested long ago upon earth has been delayed solely by man and through no fault of the Father, whose kingdom is still in the process of coming! Today the cosmic wheel has turned almost to the point of no return, and it is imperative for all mankind that the necessary unity and other divine qualities be forthcoming with expediency....

"Recently the Darjeeling Council, through the beloved ascended master El Morya, your friend and mine, made known the formation of a spiritual fraternity to be composed of dedicated men and women who are willing to put their shoulders, minds, and hearts to the wheel of sponsorship in the coordination of manifold activities under our direction. This voluntary group of the faithful is destined, if they will accept it, to be a part of the selective focus from which shall be drawn the permanent focus of beloved El Morya's Diamond Heart (dedicated to the will of God) in the outer world of form. Now I am honored to acknowledge the first tangible gleams from the hearts of those blessed ones who have accepted with dignity and joy the real privilege of becoming Keepers of the Flame."[1]

The Keepers of the Flame

In his letter dated January 31, 1961, beloved El Morya stated:

"I am therefore authorizing the formation of a specially dedicated group within The Summit Lighthouse to be made up of actual members of good standing. This is to be called the Keepers of the Flame.... To this end class lessons are to be offered to the members of the Keepers of the Flame group. Regardless of one's station, all those interested in both basic and advanced instruction ought to enroll in this dedicated group of servers for many reasons. A word to the wise is sufficient."

The Mother of the Flame

At the time The Summit Lighthouse was established, there was also established the office of the Mother of the Flame as a part of the Keepers of the Flame Fraternity founded by the ascended master Saint Germain. That great honor was bestowed upon me by the master to keep the Flame of Life with the Maha Chohan, the Representative of the Holy Spirit, who is the Keeper of the Flame of all Life. I was almost overwhelmed when I realized what it meant.

"Because one among you ought to be selected to symbolize

constancy and because I cannot practically select everyone as an honored figurehead of constancy, I am leaving all others to choose for themselves to emulate the quality and in such a manner receive the fullness of its cosmic honor. Yet as a symbol I am choosing from my heart one who truly loves God and the blessed Chohans with a love almost nonpareil to be the Mother of the Flame. I nominate for this high honor Miss Louise Kieninger, directing also that a biography of her interesting life to the present be compiled so that it may be read by students of Truth everywhere."[2]

The Light of God never fails. For years I had given in my early class decrees for all mankind, the youth and incoming lifestreams, the government, America, and the planet. I would intensify my decrees. I knew that every lifestream on this planet has the Flame of Life (God) in his heart, also a ministering angel (sometimes called a guardian angel, given us at the first embodiment on this planet), and that this angel remains with each lifestream until he has fulfilled his divine plan and returned to God to go out no more.

One Father: One God

To God we are truly brothers and sisters, no matter who we are or how we spend Life's energy. I learned then to see in the heart of each lifestream the Flame of God and to send my love to that flame (God) and to the ministering angel. It was not always easy, but I know achievement is not without effort.

It is easy to express opinions on things that are not our business and to criticize. I know God never criticizes; the ascended masters never criticize; the angels never criticize. It is easy to ask God to forgive them, for they know not what they are doing. The great masters are so willing to help us if we ask them.

The Summit Lighthouse publication *Pearls of Wisdom* is the weekly letter of instruction direct from the masters. It is truly a priceless pearl. The Keepers of the Flame Lessons are also full of instruction and information from the ascended masters, as are the many booklets, pamphlets, and the ascended masters' magnificent dictations, all shared with students.

During this time my sister, who lived in the West, was in an automobile accident—not too serious, but she required hospitalization. I felt I would like to be with her. She was a widow and had no children. Her home was two stories; she gave me the second floor. I set up a beautiful shrine and held my class every morning at five, including Mother Mary's class for purification of the homes, the families, and especially the mothers, friends, teachers, and guardians of the incoming children, the younger generation, and the youth of the world.

Soon the home became too much for her to care for, and she sold it. We arranged a comfortable home for her, and I returned east to a conference of The Summit Lighthouse in Washington. During this time two of the staff members and I were invited to lunch in the congressional cafeteria. During lunch the thought came to me, Why not magnetize the Light in the halls of Congress? The young men were delighted. Our hostess returned to business and we started. It was summertime and Congress was not in session. We had the House and Senate chambers to ourselves. We magnetized them with the Sacred Flame. We did it, of course, quietly. We did the same as we walked through the Capitol building. This ritual has become a part of my morning class.

Constancy

In an early letter, beloved El Morya says that constancy is the first quality of a Keeper of the Flame and is the greatest quality next to love needed to maintain a focus for God. In every balance of life, no matter how versatile in endowment or how broad the culture, there is a grand central purpose in which all the subordinate powers of the soul are brought to a focus and where they will find expression.

Beloved El Morya says: "True it is that the Path leading to the Summit is fraught at times with peril. In the past, many did not seem able to procure the stamina or faith to reach or to remain at the almost dizzying heights; yet with pride stifled and the Presence of God I AM as your staff, you can do as we did and climb for yourself the narrow stairs that lead to the little upper room in the tower of The Summit Lighthouse, where you will help to keep the Flame which represents this activity burning now and in all days to come."[3]

The Dream of God for the Summit

The messenger's article which appeared in the *Summit Beacon* of November 1965 gives God's dream for the Summit. It is mine also, and I quote it here for all who follow after me as sons and daughters of the Flame:

"Goal-fitting is the science of *knowing* where you are *going*. The joyous angels of Christmas once sang, 'Glory to God in the highest,' and so now we present this brief capsule of God's dream for the Summit of man's being whereby he may ever reach for the light emanating from the Father's house.

"The Summit is practical. Builded upon the bedrock of Christed intelligence, it accepts the best in life, in religion, in science, in the humanities, in just plain people who love God and desire to dream with Him of a better world as an ever-present reality.

"The masters need a focus through which they may funnel their energies to mankind; we seek to provide a cup of communion offered from below to our Brothers on high whereby we might receive and retain the oil of divine love, facility, and peace. By this mutual endeavor mankind unascended may find the road that leads upward, defying the downward trends of gravity, rising gently but firmly at varying paces. For some the Summit provides chambers of solitude for moments of quiet thought, and for others the soul-shaking impetus of God's Word made manifest for today.

"Neither Rome nor the New Jerusalem are builded in a day. Ours is the work of the swiftly flying moments, the days, the years, and even the centuries. The Summit is continually being organized by Higher Intelligences to open the way for a massive spiritual exodus out of the delusions of the present and all past ages. It seeks the bounty of freedom for every man, either in the lofty pursuit of his own religion or in the 'coming apart' to be a separate people wholly dedicated to the Summit experiences of life.

"The name Summiteer was given by one of our members as descriptive of those who seek the experience of total reunion with God, which can only be attained as men *will* to leave the false landmarks and rise to the very heights of their own God-potential. There is a niche for all in the Summit, just as in the sunlight of Truth there is a place for all the rays; those helpers who wish to give a hand to others on the Path find their reward through the Summit that leads Home to peace, progress, and power restored.

"There is a place for those who need help, instruction, healing, and an outworking together of love which transcends the shattering impact of diverse doctrines, religious speculation and casuistry.

"Here all can assemble under the canopy of one God to seek and to find that glory to God in the highest which is the Summit of every man—the search, the seeker, and the attainment merging into self-transcending planes of Identity. The veils part and new hope is born as one incorporates the written or spoken Word released in the ever-present Now from the ascended masters' realm.

"The Summit is a dream of union with God, whom we have not wholly seen, for he transcends every attempt to capture his beauty. The Summit is the dream of God in man, God's dream of reflected victory—that which is above manifesting below as hope which spurs men on until each victory won completes some phase of his immaculate design.

"An eternal goal is the Summit dream of God, organized in human consciousness and among men solely for the purposes of dissemination of truth and cosmic education, solely for amalgamation of heart with heart as a union of hope which teaches divine friendship to both child and child-man.

"This is but a glimpse of the Summit. Much is still hidden from our eyes; but God is revealing His plan day by day, from glory unto glory, even by his Spirit."

I would like to share with you an excerpt from an address given by beloved Casimir Poseidon, who, as an ascended being, ruled an ancient civilization which existed from twelve to fourteen thousand years ago near the Amazon. His counsel to the people was "Learn to love to do well, and you shall!" Under his guidance the culture reached great heights of achievement, for "it was an age of peace, and progress was the order of the day."

"Now then, as the ceremony is being performed by your own beloved Saint Germain and a certain quality is being radiated to your messengers, I call to your attention that they are made a prince and princess of this holy order of the God and Goddess Meru, and a crown of illumination is placed upon their brow according to the fulfillment of the divine decree.

"I do not deny that they, as all mankind, must live up to this high standard by right action; but I pray that all of you, rather than tear down mankind, will tear down no one, but will lift these individuals up and help them to hold their destiny when the powers of the human world seek to tear from them—as they seek to tear from yourselves, each and every one—the crown of Life which God seeks to bestow.

"You need to help one another, precious ones, not to hinder one another. You need to hold the divine image of the Overcomer for one another. You need to recognize that each day you have a means offered to you whereby you can serve Life. Each day opportunities come; and when you fail to accept them or to recognize them, it is not because God wills it so; it is not because you will it so, in many cases; but it is because you do not summon the faith and you do not summon the power to overcome the confining aspects of your being, to overthrow the egotistical outer self, but you continue to think in terms of personal good, when the greatest personal good of all comes about as you give yourself to God and the fulfillment of his destiny.

"Ladies and gentlemen, because we desire to see mankind master their emotional worlds, we have this day brought forth this accomplishment as an activity of the Great White Brotherhood for the further enhancing of Life on this planet.

"Rejoice and be glad, for the kingdom cometh when every man shall indeed be a king and every woman a queen because God sits upon the throne of their hearts. And where God sits, there the reign of peace and security exists in the infinite law of the circle, not in the broken human law of the dotted line.

"I thank you, and I bid you a pleasant good afternoon."[4]

One Nation under God

My heart moves with the kindling spirit of the Founding Fathers, of George Washington, whose unswerving devotion to freedom and to obedience to the law carved for him the opportunity to embody as the beloved messenger Godfré Ray King. It was through his mission that I came to know Saint Germain and to have an appreciation for the Flame that is America. These words from the *Summit Beacon* express my sentiments:

"Let us build this nation under God of that substance which endures. Thus shall America remain forever the land of the free. Thus shall her torch be an immortal fagot, a fount of flame to which all nations may come and kindle and rekindle virtue and good will for the brotherhood of man under the Fatherhood of God."[5]

The years of my retirement have been happy and busy in the service of the Light. Every Saturday afternoon we ask the great hosts of heaven to magnify all cathedrals, churches, shrines, missions—all places of worship in America and the world—with the Sacred Fire of love, peace, harmony, and victory.

The success most precious to our hearts is to truly know that we are doing God's will to the best of our ability. No other can know this as well as we ourselves. Its meaning is to measure up to the divine standard and await the words from on high "Well done."

Jesus' Watch

[Editor's note: Beloved Clara Louise was embodied as the Apostle James, who, with Peter and John, saw Jesus transfigured and was with him in the garden vigil. In her final embodiment, of which she wrote these memoirs, she was devoted to Jesus; and when he initiated the Watch-with-Me-One-Hour Service, she became his ardent supporter, giving the Watch daily on behalf of earth's evolutions. Thus she requested that the following quote from the Watch be included in her book.]

"And he cometh unto the disciples and findeth them asleep and saith unto Peter, *What! could ye not watch with me one hour?* Watch and pray, that ye enter not into temptation; the spirit indeed is willing, but the flesh is weak."[6]

"For centuries, followers of Christ have felt remorse for the disciples that they did not keep the vigil with Jesus as he prayed in the garden during the hours before his betrayal and crucifixion. Perhaps some have thought, 'If only I had been there, I might have helped our Lord.' Others look for an opportunity in their daily activities to be steadfast in the calling, realizing that his watch is perpetual to the present hour.

"Remembering the hours when his heart was heavy for the burdens of the world, Jesus has offered in this day and age to watch with mankind as they go through the trials and tests that were his to pass. The following service was dictated by Jesus in actual manifestation. It is his offering to a world still fraught with chaos, war, pride, superstition, and ignorance. Through it mankind today may pledge their love and faithfulness to watch with Jesus one hour each week as an atonement for those who have failed to do so and in commemoration of those who throughout all ages to come will keep the faith.

"Today, followers of all religions still believe that the answer to every problem may be found with God. Prayer is the open door through which all blessings flow. It is the avenue of Light betwixt heaven and earth. It is talk with God; it is supplication; it is the yearning of the heart. Through prayer mankind's consciousness is mellowed: fears are assuaged as he gains strength, a greater sense of the Infinite, and his own place in God's scheme of things. People the world over become one as they lay their all upon the altar of prayer and they feel the wondrous joy of the Christ who continues to walk with men; they feel the power of the Holy Spirit and they know that their Redeemer liveth.

"Those who remember the many admonishments of the great Master Physician, who healed every form of sin, disease, and even death, may have concepts of truth concerning his doctrine which are not necessarily the fullness of all that he has prepared for his flock in this day and age. His promise to those he left behind was 'Verily, verily, I say unto you, He that believeth on me, *the works that I do shall he do also; and greater works than these shall he do;* because I go unto my Father.'[7] If men are to follow Christ's example and then do even greater works, greater understanding must come forth. Christians today must be willing to accept the progressive revelation of the Christ as His Law applies to the problems of the twentieth century and to the battle of Armageddon in which we are engaged.

"Throughout the ages progress has come forth in science, in art, and in every area of culture; yet men are reticent to believe that religion, too, must be progressive. When men search for the ultimate and then are convinced they have found it, they close the door to the continuous outpouring of revelation from the Heart of God, who gives to each one according to his capacity to receive."[8]

Liberty Proclaims

I would like to quote now the words of the Goddess of Liberty. By way of explanation of the office of Cosmic Being and spokesman for the Karmic Board, I quote the messengers' introduction to her dictations printed in their book entitled *Liberty Proclaims:*

"'I lift my lamp beside the golden door' are the God-inspired words upon the Statue of Liberty in New York City's harbor. This colossal Statue of Liberty means far more to every man, woman, and child upon this planet than a salute from France by way of several freedom-loving French statesmen and one freedom-dedicated sculptor, Auguste Bartholdi. This symbol of freedom from political and religious tyrannies is far more than a man-inspired edifice of concrete and steel produced after many years of frustrated planning and of slow subscription drives for the monied man's thousands and the widow's freely given mite—mingled monies of both France and America—mingling as two blood streams that flow into one heart to pulse life into a seemingly inanimate monument.

"The world-famous Statue of Liberty which guards our

shores and is a much more powerful protection to our entire nation than any unascended being may realize and which is honored in fervent song and verse is the likeness of the beloved Goddess of Liberty—that radiant being of light and divine love who is the guardian spirit of our nation.

"Not only was America—the 'golden door of opportunity'—designed in the ascended masters' realm, but so was the idea of placing the magnificent Statue of Liberty in one of America's greatest harbors preordained by the higher powers. America had been selected by divine plan long ago to hold the heart of the Light of freedom for the entire planet; and the statue, unveiled in 1886, was the visual focus for the strong in heart, the brave of spirit, the 'tired', the 'poor', the 'huddled masses yearning to breathe free.'[9]

"The Goddess of Liberty's statue carries a book—the Book of Divine Law—and wears a crown of seven rays, symbolic of the seven mighty Elohim of creation, who represent divine will, wisdom, love, purity, healing, ministration, and ordered service. About the statue's feet are chains; but the chains are broken, symbolizing a being free from bondage who is stepping forth to enlighten the world. And to enlighten the world is indeed the beloved Goddess of Liberty's intent. Her torch is the flame of divine illumination lighting the way for millions groping in the darkness of their own human creation and effluvia, lighting the way to divine freedom, to liberty, to the only Reality—oneness with God...."[10]

The words of Mother Liberty are a thrill to my soul even now as I behold her golden aura from the sun:

"From His Light I came and to His Light I return. And as I go, I wish to stimulate in each of you your spiritual eye in order that you may feel the pulsations of the fire of Jove (so-called in mythology) from the sky, the power of Love that pulsates as the single eye of vision.

O catch its gleams,
Like the Holy Grail of old,
And know that it contains
The elixir whose wonders are untold.

The splendor of the ages
Is herein revealed
And not concealed,
For God is in thy frame,
And by the power of His Flame,
You shall rise in ascension's name,
Your beloved Jesus to claim,
Your beloved Saint Germain to adore.
The power of God's Light forevermore
Will be your own,
And you will be my son, my daughter,
Of love not yet known, but hoped for.

Unafraid, I come.
And in the power of Love I move,
And I give to all the great radiance of my love.
Who will hear our voice
And receive our radiance?
Who will listen when we speak
And be stirred more than an hour?
Who will feel the great surge of our power
And hold that inviolate throughout life
Until Heaven be gained?

Herein is no strain,
But only the gentle relaxation of falling rain,
The heavenly rain descending
Upon the parched ground of mankind's lack
And bringing the flowers of heaven
    into manifestation.

They spring up, they rise, they pulsate
With resurrection's power,
And the feet of the Christ are pressed
Into the soft, moist earth.

Mankind walking in His name,
In His image, in His Flame,
Are comforted by God's name,
Which I AM manifesting.[11]

My life has always been the will of God first; and if there was time left, then the necessities of the hour. When I met the masters, I knew I had found the source of the inspiration of my love for God's will—El Morya, the champion not only of this will, but of the Light of Mother Mary and the fervor of Saint Germain for the freedom of America:

"As the cycles of the years turn and the fires of hope are stirred and rekindled again and again, there comes a time in the tides of each man's life when he must stir, with gratitude, the fires of liberty.

"Liberty cradled America's head on the bosom of God and, through countless outreachings by the masses of this great land, sought to dispense not only good but also the Word of God, which the progenitors of America were wont to emblazon on the hearts of its people as upon the coins of the realm, 'In God We Trust.'

"Through days of peril in past times, the hand of God has been seen silently outworking a destiny of honor and hope for the people of all lands through the heart of America. The search was intended to be dual; but while God has continuously sought the hearts of His people everywhere upon earth through the integral interpretation of 'liberty for all,' all have not sought him. The dark pall of atheism, of skepticism, and of doubt has crept in again and again to dampen and destroy the hopes of men, barring the doorway to progress of soul and enclosing men in the sordid limitations of sense consciousness.

"The old refrain 'Mine eyes have seen the glory of the coming of the Lord' from the 'Battle Hymn of the Republic' has been heard less and less, and the light of the candle of God has burned less and less in the rooms of the youth of America and the world."[12]

The Light of God Never Fails

The Light of God never fails. It has never failed me and will not fail anyone who trusts in it and remains calm. I have never sought a position. As I finished one position, the door was open to another.

Coming home from Italy one time, we crossed the Mediterranean Sea. It was always my wish to really see it. It was a beautiful day, the sea blue-calm. There were not many passengers. The airplanes were not as large then as now. I decided to change my seat to one on the opposite side. After a few moments the window where I had been sitting flew open. I felt no fear; I knew the Light of God never fails. I thought for a moment that if we were to go down, we would go into that beautiful water. The window was soon closed and we traveled on.

Another time on my way from New York to Topeka to attend the funeral of my niece, I noticed one of the propellers of the plane had stopped and the plane had lessened speed. We were late, of course, when we arrived in Kansas City. The next plane was at 7:00 p.m. The funeral was at 11:00 a.m. I said to the clerk, "What will I do?" The plane had left, and I told him what my mission was. He said: "There is a Greyhound bus out of Kansas City about this time for the West. I will phone and see if they will hold it for you." And they did.

We arrived at my sister's home just as she was locking the door. The limousine was waiting for her. She unlocked the door, the chauffeur put the suitcase in the living room, and we went off. Again, the Light of God never fails.

During the Second World War, I was again going West. Getting a seat in a plane was almost impossible. I arrived at 7:00 a.m. in Kansas City. The plane to Topeka was to leave at 7:00 p.m. and no seats were available. We were to report every hour to see if there were any vacancies. At noon I received an invitation from the manager of the beautiful dining room to be a guest for luncheon with a paid ticket up to $2.50. I used only a small part of the ticket and returned it to the cashier with a written thank you. I went again to see if there was a vacancy. There was a colonel in the line and one person between us—no vacancies.

When the colonel stepped up to get his ticket, he was graciously received by the clerk. "We have your reservation," said he to the colonel. The colonel replied, "Give that ticket to the young woman." The clerk started to remonstrate. The colonel answered, "I am a colonel of the United States Army, and I am not accustomed to having my orders questioned." The clerk gave the ticket to me. And all through my life it was that way. The Light of God never fails. And it never will if we have calmness and faith.

I close my memoirs with the blessings of Mother Mary:

"Between the dark and the daylight of human consciousness, there is a hunger that, like a hidden spring from within the fold of consciousness, reaches out to understand the mysteries of Life, the mysteries of resurrection, the mysteries of my Son's offering and realization. What a pity it is that men and women are prone to sell short their immortal birthright and to consider that they are unworthy of the calling of Christ Identity.

"With the world in such a state of turmoil and all of heaven striving to bring forth the beauty of the abundant Life, men and women need as never before fellowship with Truth—to sit at the feet of the Masters of Wisdom and to renew themselves in those things spiritual. Life, real Life, is not temporal. It is eternal; and it stems from the eternal radiance of perfection, the perfect Life of God that seeks to manifest in men."[13]

I had learned well the Light of God never fails and the power of silence. My love and gratitude are beyond words to express. I had found that for which I had been searching—The Summit Lighthouse.

CHAPTER 13

The Promise of the Ascension

Acting in the authority of her office of Mother of the Flame, Clara Louise Kieninger conducted a vigil for youth Monday evening, July 2, 1962, at Saint Germain's Freedom Class in Washington, D.C. She conducted songs and decrees for and on behalf of the youth of the world, the incoming children, their parents and teachers. After her two-hour service, Mother Mary gave through Mark a dictation in which she announced the promise of the Great Divine Director that Clara Louise would ascend at the close of this her final embodiment of service to mankind. The dictation follows.

Be still, my children, and know that the I AM in you is God. Your keeping of this vigil with me has meant more than your outer self may know. It has meant a manifestation of the Christ Consciousness for some yet unborn; and for others who are leaving this planet, it means the difference between their freedom or their remaining in bondage.

I come tonight with a very short message; but I choose to enfold you in such love that as you sleep tonight in the consciousness of the arms of the Father Presence around you, you shall know that you are sustained by a mother's heart.

And so, beloved one [Mother Mary speaks directly to Clara Louise Kieninger], thou who hast served so long, may thine eyes be touched as the stars from heaven. For unto thee at the close of this embodiment, the Great Divine Director has told me, shall come thy ascension. This has been promised to thee for the faithfulness of thy service to the Light. And it is as sure as the starry path that leads back to the heart of God—the shining Light.

And thou shalt meet first Serapis Bey, thy teacher; and then I shall stand and say to thee, "Welcome Home, thou Mother of the Flame, to the heart of God—to go no more out, to remain forever in the heart of the Eternal One, and to do his eternal will." [Beloved Clara Louise Kieninger addresses the messenger, "May I kiss your hand for her?" The messenger Mark L. Prophet extends his hand, and the Mother of the Flame kisses it in honor of Mother Mary.] The gift that has been given, the service rendered, is done in the holy name of the Christ of everyone—my Son, your brother.

And now I thank you all for the offering of yourselves to me within the silent recesses of your heart. In the stillness of the night, realize that in the so-called mystic Light of God that shines from yon distant stars there is a unity and oneness, threads of Light weaving together a comprehensible union of many hearts of Light. You are one—E Pluribus Unum, E Pluribus Unum—one out of many. And like the stars in the flag of this blessed nation, you can make your lives sublime and leave behind you those precious footsteps in the sands immortal, sands of Light.

Thank you and good night.

Washington, D.C.
July 3, 1962
1:00 A.M. E.D.T.

The Reward of the Mother of the Flame

Clara Louise Kieninger made her ascension, as Mother Mary had said she would, from Berkeley, California, on October 25, 1970. The mantle of the office of the Mother of the Flame had been transferred to the messenger Elizabeth Clare Prophet on April 9, 1966. On that day Elizabeth received the scepter and the ring of the Mother of the Flame and Clara Louise became Regent Mother of the Flame, an office which she still holds as the ascended lady master Clara Louise.

In Gautama Buddha's annual New Year's address on January 1, 1973, Clara Louise was present at inner levels throughout the service. Gautama spoke of the return of her youthful appearance in her ascended state and announced that she would present to the Mother of the Flame a torch of illumination to the age:

"As I stand here addressing you then this evening, it is my desire to acquaint you with a circumstance concerning your own activity here in Santa Barbara, in Colorado Springs, and in many parts of the world. Some of you may recall one who passed from you some time ago, the first Mother of the Flame who later became the Regent Mother. Well, I want you to know that tonight at inner levels she is with you. Her name upon earth, Louise Kieninger, will kindle in many of you a response of her great love.

"I want you to understand that her body is no longer gray or crooked in any way; her form no longer reflects age, but only the beauty of her earliest youth and maturity. Upon her face there is a glow of hope and sweetness and love. Her keynote is indeed that which was played to you upon the violin this very evening, 'Calm As the Night.'

"I want you to know that she will be with you until this service shall break up. Until you shall leave and depart these doors, she will be with you this night, giving her love and her counsel at inner levels to you, conveying her blessing to you as the first Mother of the Flame. And she shall, ere the night pass, give to the present Mother of the Flame *a torch charged with the vital fires from God's heavenly altar and the conveyance of a vast mission to illumine the world's children and produce the blessing of true culture to the age and unto all people everywhere.*

"Is this then not a great blessing to those of you who can understand it—and even to those who cannot? It is the conveyance of a soul into its higher octave of light, into the ritual of its ascension. Do you understand, then, that as this goal that was once given to her and promised unto her by Mary the Mother of Jesus herself has been achieved and fulfilled, this blessed soul desires that you should feel the currents of her love even now? And heaven itself asks that the angels that accompany me, the beautiful devas, will fold their wings, as it were, in adoration to her Divine Presence."

Thus from the hand of the Buddha through the hand of the messenger, Elizabeth received the torch from the ascended Clara Louise. Two months later Mark made his ascension on February 26, 1973, and Elizabeth assumed the responsibility for directing the expansion of the ascended masters' teachings throughout the world. By fall she was teaching over seventy students at the newly founded ascended masters' university in Santa Barbara. On the anniversary of Clara Louise's ascension, as the students paid tribute to that great and noble lady and concluded the day's lectures with a meditation to "Calm As the Night," Louise came forth to deliver her first dictation from the ascended state. We include it for all who loved her on earth, that they might also love her in heaven.

CHAPTER 14

In the Twinkling of an Eye

    I come in the flame of Mary, Mother of all, whose energies nourished and sustained me during my final service on earth. It was, precious hearts, a service that I gladly rendered, even while my soul yearned for the great homing, the great homecoming, the reunion with God and my own twin flame.

    As the years of my service passed and I saw the generations of mankind move in and out of war and the little ones grow up in an atmosphere of discord, disease, and disturbance to the inner patterns of the soul, I learned to walk with Jesus, continuing the walk on the road to Emmaus.[1] I called him brother then and I call him brother now.

    As we serve together in the Temple of the Resurrection, it is for the sustaining of the immaculate grace of the Cosmic Virgin in mothers upon earth, in souls coming into embodiment to give their final hours of service as they, too, prepare for the ascension. Thus it is with great love that I behold your efforts in the Community of the Holy Spirit and your efforts to present yourselves a living sacrifice[2] to make yourself ready to be the recipient of these souls that are descending.

I have been privileged to walk with the Great Divine Director; and in my service to the Cosmic Virgin, he has allowed me to behold the pristine pattern of their soul-identity. And he has asked that I continue my service, service to the Flame as the Regent Mother of the Flame, not only on behalf of souls in embodiment, but on behalf of those souls who have never taken embodiment in the world of form. And thus a portion of my daily communion with Omega is to reinforce the Christic pattern of the seventh root race within the consciousness of those parents who are destined to bring forth the seventh-root-race children.

Some of these parents are in embodiment in this hemisphere, North and South America; and some are yet abiding in etheric temples waiting to be born, that they might bring forth these souls twenty years from now, twenty-five years, thirty years. And thus by giving birth to souls who are preparing, you see, you can entertain unawares the parents of the seventh root race and become thereby grandparents of these incoming souls.

And you will live to see them. And when you find yourselves at that age when you can enjoy your grandchildren, you will see by your heightened sensitivity, which you will have gained by that time by your devotion to the Flame, that the auras of these precious ones will have a violet hue, and their rosy cheeks and their delicate skin tone will also have a violet cast. And in those days you will remember that on October 25, 1973, as I came to you to establish the victory of my ascension and to lock you in my embrace, you heard my words and my prophecy of those who would come forth.

You see, precious hearts, it will take several centuries before the entire seventh root race is in embodiment. They will come in sections according to the rays under which they serve. The forerunners of the seventh root race are the strong who have etched upon their etheric bodies the flame of God's holy will. They come imbued with that power to clear the way, to establish the right consciousness of the holy will. And so, you see, in the focus of God's holy will which you have dedicated, you are likewise reinforcing the will of God on behalf of the forerunners, the avant-garde of the seventh root race.

And next will come those who serve on the second ray, and then the third, fourth, fifth, sixth and seventh. And in this order and by this divine design, the Great Divine Director will sponsor the lifewave. And you will see the pattern of that lifewave at inner levels be as a giant curve until the focal point of the curve, like the trailing garments of the comet itself,* will manifest centrally in the Son consciousness. And the Christ consciousness of the seventh root race will come to the fore, then, when each of the members of that race serving on each of the seven rays shall have come into embodiment.

You must also understand that light descends and that waves of light come forth within the first wave as representatives of all of the seven rays are within the first wave. And thus you see that spirals within spirals within spirals prepare the way for the grand finale of the entire mandala of a root race to appear.

I come then with hope in my heart and with a desire to see the healing of the Mother of the Flame, of each son and daughter of the Flame, of all that would impede the flow of light. Karmic conditions can be dissolved; impediments that have existed from childhood can be no more. I will assist you to restore within yourself, within each one. But remember, the call must precede the answer. Yet before you have called, I have answered, saith the Lord.[3] And the answer that comes forth is to the call of the soul before it even reaches the outer mind.

There is a spiral of victory that is anchored in the atmosphere over the place where I made my ascension. And therefore, I shall direct you to that place and to that home, that you might ever

---

* The comet Kohoutek heralded the descent of the 10,001 avatars to be born in coming months.

know when you are in the area of Berkeley that there is a focus which blesses and heals and is sustained for the little ones. And by your application to that focus, you can expand the influence of the Archangel Gabriel and Hope, of the Goddess of Purity,* throughout this state, throughout America and the world.

For wherever and whenever a devotee of light ascends, there is always the influence that settles in the etheric plane; and as the earth spins upon its axis, that influence also makes a circle of fire around the planetary body. And thus many lives are blessed; and your consciousness also has been blessed by that focus and by the focuses of many others who have ascended from the planet earth.

I would call to your attention and to those of you who knew me while I walked among you that I had, as it were, a thorn in the flesh, as Saint Paul might say.[4] And that thorn was an impediment in my eyesight. And toward the latter years of my service, it was difficult for me to go out because of this impediment in my sight. I bring this to your attention that you may know that by working out karmic patterns collectively for the planet as well as individually, you may share in the mission of the Saviour who came to heal the sins of the world, to bear those sins that mankind might have a greater opportunity to manifest the light.

And thus in the twilight years, I bore this infirmity which taught me humility before God. And in the bearing of that imperfect state in my flesh, I came to honor the perfect state of God in man, and my consciousness came to be more and more centered in the Christ. And thus a greater love and compassion for my fellowman, for those who were not perfect of form, enveloped me. And I am grateful to the Lords of Karma for teaching me this lesson; for every lesson that is learned before the

---

* The etheric retreat of Archangel Gabriel and Hope is located between Sacramento and Mount Shasta, California. The Goddess of Purity maintains a focus over the city of San Francisco.

ascension is of so much more value after the ascension, for it leaves a record whereby the ascended one may return to the scene of that lesson and give that lesson to others on the Path.

And so as I speak to you of this teaching, I can also impart to you the record of my evolving consciousness and how out of humility and how out of the acceptance of the imperfections of the flesh I became hallowed and blessed by the perfections of the Spirit. And I learned to desire not so much the perfectionment of the physical body, lest pride should overtake me in the thought of perfecting the form; but I came to desire the perfection of the soul. And above all, I prized my nearness with God, my closeness to Mother Mary, to her flame, to being like unto her, a cosmic virgin on behalf of earth's evolutions.

Therefore, consider then, as you meditate upon healing, that your desire for healing of yourself or of another self be not rooted in pride—either the pride to be thought among the spiritual elect or those who have extraordinary powers from the Godhead or the pride to be perfect in the physical form, which is the pride of the Luciferians. Take care when you invoke healing that the motive of healing be that God be glorified in man, that the will of God be reestablished by the action of the healing thought form, and most important, that through healing, the soul experiences the alchemical union with the Spirit through gratitude, through love, through praise.

Thus bear your infirmities, bear the infirmities of one another until you know that the hour is come to make the necessary call for healing. And then pray first for the healing of human pride, of human stubbornness and willfulness, of selfishness. Desire to be rid of these, and you will see how your countenance and your form will be molded after the heavenly virtues which descend into the void that is left when pride and rebellion and selfishness are dissolved in the fervent heat of your love for God and man. And so, you see, this is really not a roundabout way of healing, but it is the direct course to become established in God. And once God sees that you have made your desire his desire, then all these things will be added unto you.[5]

I stand before you in a youthful body of light. I appear to you as I was at the age of sixteen—with perfect sight and hearing, the gift of Cyclopea and my own I AM Presence. Thus the glory of God that is upon my countenance is the love that I have sent forth to my Creator which He has returned to me. And thus I am but a reflector of the Image Most Holy, the mirror of God, selfless. Standing in the place of the Most High God, one cannot retain any vestige of self that is not the Self of God; and this is the test and the meaning of the ascension.

You ascend when your divine plan is fulfilled in selflessness. And the synthetic image is dissolved, the Real Image appears, and you discover and you proclaim, "I AM the Real Self in action evermore!" This is the ascension in the light. And before many years or many decades pass, I know that I shall count from among these numbers the numbers of the heavenly hosts who gather to celebrate the victory and the total submergence in the light and the emergence into the light of each son and daughter of God.

And so as I arose on that day from the earth, the very earth that you now walk and of which your bodies are composed, I rose like an arrow, clothed with ascension's fires, as Serapis Bey came to that place to honor that place where the Mother flame had been enshrined, to establish a focus of the ascension currents for all time. And I arose through the densities, the maya, and the illusion of mankind's consciousness into the air, as my soul took leave of that body temple, higher and higher into the rarefied atmosphere of the etheric plane, robed in the garments of the Holy Spirit and in the Deathless Solar Body which had been woven of my prayers and invocations to the Mother and into the Presence of the Christ and of the I AM.

Coming into that forcefield, it was like the locking of my soul into eternal perfection. And I felt the translation as the shifting of gears from one state of limitation to the state of limitless perfection. And thus I am the living, eternal witness of the fiat of the last trump sounding, of the twinkling of an eye, of the moment when death is swallowed up in victory.[6]

And I can truly say to you that although the hours, the days, the weeks and months and years of preparation seemed long, at the moment when God called me Home, it was in the twinkling of an eye that I was made whole and that I returned to the wholeness of being. And I saw and I heard celestial choirs singing the keynote which you have graciously played to me this day, "Calm As the Night." And I heard the music as from my own abode, from my own mansion, my Causal Body of light. And I heard it from the Causal Body of my twin flame. And I saw, as it were, the heavens filled with smiling faces, with cherubim and seraphim, and with many souls who had been healed and uplifted by my prayers.

And thus so great were the rewards—all in that twinkling of an eye—I could only stand and pour forth gratitude to Serapis Bey, to Mother Mary, to Jesus, to the great Spirit of the eternal Mother and of the great Brotherhood of lightbearers. Thus will that day come for each one of you who will determine to keep in the way of the Mother of the Flame, in the way of purity and of the ascension spiral. All things are possible if you *will* with God to make them possible.[7]

I leave you with the fragrance of the rose of the ascension from the Temple of Luxor, the white rose of Mary. And I leave you with that floral offering, and I place it in your hands now, each one. Even as the disciples received the gift of the white rose and the white lilies in the tomb of Mary, so I desire when you open the tomb of God's consciousness that you shall behold there the testimony of the victory of one soul, one devotee of the

Divine Mother. And in that witness, which was given to Thomas, you may also know that what man has done, man can do. What one soul has accomplished, every soul can accomplish.

I AM in the I AM Presence of each one of you; and in that Presence, I AM like unto thyself. When I walked the earth, I was no different from any of you in potential. But I took the law as the affirmation of victory, and I applied the law and I practiced it. And with practice, lo, I AM perfect! With practice, lo, you also can be, and you are, perfect.

I AM with you as you strive for the immaculate conception of each incoming child and for the healing arts and the spirit of nursing. I AM your Mother on the Path.

The Motherhouse
Santa Barbara, California
October 25, 1973
4:23 P.M. P.D.T.

The Spirit of Nursing, a sculpture by R. Tait MacKenzie
American Red Cross Building, Washington, D.C.

A Victory of Life

Now in the Spirit of the Resurrection, I come to bring comfort to life in this cycle of the year when spirals of disintegration carry some among mankind through the ritual of transition to other octaves of consciousness. I come with comfort; and I come to bring peace to hearts yearning for the flame of the Prince of Peace—my brother, my master, and my friend.

I come on the light of victory, the victory over the last enemy,[8] to define what some among mankind call death and to redefine that concept. For it is, you see, the working-out of mankind's own acceptance of the laws of mortality. Mankind affirm that all good things must come to an end; and they conceive of life as a finite line beginning with birth, ending with death. And because they have so defined existence, so they experience death as the perversion of the flow of creation from the all-seeing eye and from the hierarchy of Scorpio.

And so my ascension, which came to me not so long ago, as you know, was a victory of life for all who would one day face the test of the ten, the test of selflessness and of God-control of energy in motion as the great flow of life. All mankind ought to remember that the energies of Scorpio are for the manifestation of the victory of cycles of creativity through the sacred fire. And each time you come to that test where a little more of the self must be sacrificed for the cause of truth, you are building the foundation of your own immortality, your own conquering with the victor over hell and death. But each time you give way to selfishness, to pettiness, and to the sting of death, then you are building a spiral of disintegration whereby the atoms and cells of being must pass through the change called death because you have willed it so, because you have, through the consciousness of sin, made death the law of your being.

Therefore to follow the admonishment of Paul to put off the old man with his deeds, to put on the new man,[9] to follow his example, "I die daily,"[10] is to daily submit to the flame your consciousness of mortality, concepts of limitation wherever they assail the mind, the heart, the emotions. Let them go into the flame; and replace them with the limitless expansion of the awareness of God as law—law of eternity, law of infinity that defines your life not as a line but as a sphere, as a cycle that is never ending, originating in God, culminating in God, going forth as the outbreath, returning as the inbreath, and recycling again and again and again as the ages of cosmic expression.

So then, see your life as a sphere, and know that day by day you are marking the path of victory. The ascension is not a future event. It is now! I proclaim to you: Now is the accepted time of your salvation [self-elevation]![11] Now is the time to accept the spiral of your integration in the flame of the ascension! Now is the time to affirm: "I AM made whole! I AM the victor over hell and death! I AM the resurrection and the life! I AM the ascension in the heart of the I AM Presence!"

And so to visualize the coil of fire given by Djwal Kul[12] is a means of magnetizing to your four lower bodies ascension's fires —to draw the flame of life, to be life, to experience wholeness, to have the flow of regeneration through your consciousness, beginning in the etheric plane, for the healing of the lower bodies of all imperfections, all decay, disease, and disintegration.

And so I come with healing in my hands to impart to you, as your nurse of the sacred fire, the energy of healing, the energy of wholeness. For hierarchy is impatient! Hierarchy is looking for those among mankind who will carry the true flame of healing and not the perversion—and not the muddied green of materia medica or the psychic impostors who heal not by the energy of the Spirit, but by lower energies, which are electricities that are secondary energies not intended for the reintegration of the spirals of Alpha and Omega in the wholeness of the Christ.

And therefore hierarchy is concerned that those who run in the race with Saint Paul[13] will have the fires of healing anchored, that they might know that the victory of healing is here and now in the very ethers, ready and waiting to be lowered into form if you will but use the power of the all-seeing eye of God to anchor the immaculate conception and visualize the perfect body, the perfect organs, and the perfect flow of energy forces through those whom you contact who ask for healing prayer. You have a responsibility to see and to know the truth, to see light bombarding darkness, eliminating darkness, and anchoring there a sun of being in the place where disease or derangement seems to manifest.

And so let a vortex of light projected from your consciousness be an anchoring point in the form of those whom you would heal, those who require your ministration. See that fiery sphere anchored in the form, in the mind, wherever there is pain. And see that whirling as a fire infolding itself, whirling into the center, drawing to it the energies of God, of the I AM Presence, of the heart center, intensifying light at that point and at the same time drawing into the center of the vortex all misqualified substance, all decay, all toxins and impurities, all karmic records.

And so that vortex of light is for the healing of the four lower bodies in the etheric plane. It is an anchoring point for the dissolving of records of hardness of heart, records of death and the condemnation of the Christ. In the mental body that vortex is for the consuming of imperfect patterns, matrices of worry and doubt and fear, imperfect concepts that have been held by mankind year after year after year. So the vortex purges the light of the mind and then flushes out the impurities of the emotional body as these cycle into the center and the fire sparkles with the light.

You will notice how that fire, that white fiery flame, will turn various colors as the chemicalization of transmutation takes place. And you will know that you will have to intensify your visualization of this vortex of sacred fire until it returns to the natural crystal-white light; and therefore invocations, decrees, and fiats will assist the anchoring of that light, along with your intense visualization. See that vortex consuming imperfections in the physical form and cycling then in the four layers of being the energies of the sacred fire for the healing that maketh all mankind whole.

I come then as a spokesman for the Healing Masters, and yet I come in the flame of ministration and service. And I come to remind you that as you take up the flame of the divine nurse to care for the sick, as you stand at the bedside of those who require healing, remember the word of comfort that is the power of the spoken word. Remember the word of cheer, of love; and remember the word of discipline that will not allow the patient to descend into self-pity, sympathy, or the consciousness of death.

Speak that word of fire and of light; and let that patient know that you will not enter into responsibility for that woe, that you not will share that sympathy. No, you will answer with the compassion of the Christ, the comfort and the flame of hope. For hope springs eternal in the heart of the one who carries the flame of the Prince of Peace; and you must give the hope of life to all who are sick, to all who are in need. For life *is* eternal, life *is* triumphant!

And therefore assist the patient into the level of awareness of detachment from the form, detachment from the disease, and all-oneness in the life of God as the flame imparts life to the body of God. As soon as the patient is nonattached, then fear is released into the flame, and doubt and all records of darkness. And as these are released, the body elemental comes forth to work the perfect work of God in man; and then you are free also to project the imaging-forth of the sacred fire. And you will see how, while the patient meditates upon life and the hope of the life everlasting, you can then enter with the mind's eye the temple of being with the Christ, the Master Physician, for the implementation of the will of God.

Always remember then never to leave one who is afflicted without saying silently within the heart: "Father, into thy hands I command his being. Father, into thy hands I command this soul, this tabernacle of thy life, this threefold flame. So let life triumph and let life reign." If you do not remember all of these words, the simple fiat "Father, into thy hands I commend his being" will suffice for angelic hosts of the Christ, angel ministrants, to care for the one who is evolving in time and space. And they will tarry there as emissaries of the Holy Spirit to provide that grace and that flow and that peace for whatever the eventuality, for whatever is the will of God.

May I then bless you with the fires of healing, of ministering love, and of the ascension flame. As I enter the anniversary of my ascension in this month, in this cycle, so I give to you, if you will have it, a coil of my being, one of the layers of that fiery coil which I, too, have visualized as the permanent electrode of the magnetization of the Great Central Sun energies. So then, let a coil of my being become congruent now with you, each one, as you go forth to fulfill your vows and to make of your being and consciousness a chalice of the Holy Spirit, a chalice of healing flow, a chalice of victory through service.

I am come and I go into the flame of our Father-Mother God. I am with you always, and I am attending the hour of your ascension in the light.

The Motherhouse
Santa Barbara, California
November 10, 1974
1:35 P.M. P.S.T.

The Annunciation of the Ascension

I come on the wings of Gabriel with the annunciation of the ascension, of ascension's fires, and of the light of Hope to every living soul who will espouse the light of love—illumined, obedient, faithful to the will of God.

I come carrying the scepter of the authority of the Regent Mother of the Flame, which office I hold, keeping the flame of life for mothers and fathers and children here below. It is a diamond scepter with a twelve-pointed star. It is, as you would imagine, the scepter of your own fairy godmother.

I am come in the light of your Presence. I am come in the light of Serapis Bey to raise this scepter of my light, to quicken within you healing fires, ascension fires, and the diamond light of the will of God. I come to renew the light of truth within you that you might carry your own scepter of authority, wielding the rod of power in the truth of the spoken Word. I come to quicken the emerald fires and the crystal light reflecting those fires that you might be instruments of healing to mankind, a healing of their minds and their emotions, a healing of their bodies, a healing of the memory, that they might have revealed the blueprint of God, the mind of God, the desiring of God to be God as love, and that all of this might cycle into manifestation into the physical body.

I come to quicken that light of healing. And many of the

saints whom you know and some whom you know not accompany me, together with the angels. We bring the light of the rose of Saint Thérèse [of Lisieux] and her fragrance and the light of Mary and of Mother Cabrini and of the beloved [Pope] John XXIII. We bring the light of those who have given their offering in service in this nation and in many nations.

I come also with news of Godfre and Lotus and their renewed efforts with Saint Germain to draw into this sacred fire of the diamond of the twelve[-pointed star] those students of the I AM [movement] in whose hearts the diamond is already the manifestation of the victory of love. It is the desire of the Knight Commander that those who love the light should unite for the victory. And I come in his name. I come to plead the cause of the God of Freedom [Saint Germain] and of Portia and the Lords of Karma, who see how much more can be done for humanity when the children of the light and those who know the law unite in the flame of healing.

And there is Padre Pio, one who is also ascended, who comes to give you of the blessing of the stigmata of our Lord. And there are others that come as saints from behind the Iron Curtain. They come with the blessed Igor to pray that you will pray—and pray without ceasing, as the beloved pilgrim—for peace, for enlightenment, for freedom to those who have taken the sword of truth and who march with Hilarion, the soldiers of the Christed ones.

This is an hour for the converging of souls in the mandala of the Mother. It is an hour for healing to be focused within you as the impartation of the word of truth. This is the hour when many souls will be called to the home of God, drawn into the heart of the I AM Presence. And therefore, as Mother Mary came on that blessed night in Washington to announce my own ascension, the promise of the Great Divine Director, I come to you this night, this blessed night, to announce to you the promise of the victory of love to one of your own, the blessed and beloved Ruth Jones, who is among you now and whose time in this place will be concluded in the cycles at hand. And at the conclusion of those cycles which are appointed unto her, her blessed and beloved twin flame, the ascended Sidney [Jones], will come, as he has already come, to be at her side with Serapis Bey and your own beloved Lanello to receive into the arms of God this devotee of the sacred fire.

I place my seal upon her brow and upon her heart, for the crown of life God has already bestowed. And you who walk in her footsteps to give to the children her teaching and her love will carry that torch and that fire and that determination to be the mother and to be the father and to be the teachers of these little ones, who come with their eyes so innocent, so trusting of your love.

I come with this, the good news of the archangel—the annunciation of the ascension. As you feel even in your midst the presence of the angels of the Ascension Temple, I ask that you sing the "Triumphal March"[14] unto the I AM Presence and the soul of Ruth, singing the wedding march for the soul's alchemical marriage, the union of the soul with the I AM Presence.

In that moment of the ascension, the bridesmaids come. They come accompanied by those sons of God who bear the golden light of victory. And there are attendants in the wedding march escorting the soul into that forcefield of that fire infolding itself[15] and the rising of the ascension flame. And truly it is the wedding day of the bride of the Lamb when the ascension comes to those who have fought the good fight and won in the planes of Terra.

Beloved hearts, you have been told by Saint Germain that if you apply the Law and give your invocations diligently and serve and sacrifice and give your surrender and continue to pray without ceasing, it is possible, altogether possible in this round, to conclude this life in victory. Now I have come before you to saturate your four lower bodies and your soul with the knowledge of the victory, the sense of victory, the certain sense of victory, the very knowing within your soul that you can make it if you try, that those who have walked among you have made it because they have tried, because they have been determined, because they have kept that flame. And they have heard the motto "Keep on keeping on." They have fallen, they have failed some tests, and they have won others. But the great battle of life is to them the victory of overcoming.

I AM here, living, tangible, a witness to the immortality of your own soul. And yet among you is one who has earned the ascension, who is ready and prepared to meet the God of the I AM Presence; and there are others who have taken leave of you and from America and other nations who have fulfilled the law of the I AM Presence. And many among you, in your service to the cause, are balancing your karma day by day; and you need not be concerned of the percentages of karma, for you understand that a percentage is only a percentage. But in the final analysis we must deal with quantity, and therefore who can know the quantity of light and darkness within the individual soul except the living God? Your service rendered supremely and selflessly day by day, year in and year out, will truly have its reward.

Therefore, do not weary in well-doing but rejoice to know that the octaves glow, that the octaves are transcendent in the fires of your own I AM Presence, and that in your service you are banking those fires, giving fuel to the ascension flame. And that if you give your heart—the open door to the sacred heart of Mary, the open door to Jesus appearing to mankind, the open door to Saint Germain and to angels who will come and go, to and fro through your heart to extend the bouquet of posies and the light of the violet flame to those along life's way—you will indeed earn your victory in this round. There is not one among you who cannot win the ascension if you will follow the light in obedience and in love, in faith, in diligence, as service, sacrifice of the lesser self, and surrender of your all to the light of victory. I come with that promise, then, not only to the one but to each and every one of you who will try to be the fullness of God in manifestation twenty-four hours a day.

May I say to you, each one, that it was a privilege to serve with the messengers on earth and it is a privilege to serve with the messengers in heaven. It is a privilege to serve with the ascended masters and their chelas. From the ascended octaves, I have surveyed the world, every nook and cranny, and I have not found anywhere in the physical octave of Terra an opportunity, a joy, a teaching, a flow such as you have in this dispensation.

I come to reinforce your victory, your overcoming, your God-determination to be free. I come to seal The Summit Lighthouse and Church Universal and Triumphant and every Keeper of the Flame and every communicant in the light of my heart and in the full protection of the Great White Brotherhood and of Lord Gautama Buddha.

Let this light, let this activity be sealed now in ascension's fires. And let it remain a focus of the love of God unto mankind until all who have been called in this dispensation and all mankind have the opportunity to know the teachings of the Christ as they were truly taught, until all mankind have the opportunity to know that the victory of love is at hand as the victory of the age.

I raise my scepter and I AM the authority of the victory of ascension's fires. I will be there to welcome you, to congratulate you, and to receive you.

I am your Mother in the light of freedom.

Retreat of the Resurrection Spiral
Colorado Springs, Colorado
October 25, 1975
9:51 P.M. M.D.T.

The Central Temple of Ancient Lemuria

In the ancient days of Lemuria I too served as a priestess at the altar of the Divine Mother. I was in the central temple of Mu and there we celebrated according to the hours, hour upon hour, the piercing ray of the ruby light sheathed in white fire.

It was a mighty pillar of flame, beloved. It was a permanent flame of the Divine Mother whereby the entire continent in its golden ages was nourished and the temples in the outer extremities of Mu, also dedicated to the Mother flame, were peopled with many adepts and devotees of that fire.

By the Mother flame was all mastery of the physical octave gained. By it many took their ascensions from succeeding golden ages where they did not depart from the purity and perfection of God.

There came a time in more recent ages when the fallen angels had made their invasion of planet earth and some had taken a level of incarnation, that they began to teach the people the misuse of the Mother flame and they arranged for opposition forces to engage the people in wars of the worlds and wars defending the supremacy of the rival gods of the underworld.

Thus the misuse of the Mother flame produced horrendous and devastating effects, even at the level of nuclear weapons. And there was a desecration of the altars; and ultimately the misuse of that Light brought about, plotted by the fallen Archangel Lucifer, the murder of the highest representative of the Divine Mother in that era and the consequent sinking of the continent.

This story has been told and retold, for it has occurred in various alterations of the theme from age to age and continent to continent. So vast is the experience and the observation of souls who have lived long upon earth that at inner levels millions now in embodiment are aware of the treacherous ways of fallen angels and how they have brought down the best and highest opportunity for souls to achieve the victory. [This they have done] by tearing down from the foundation those empires raised up by ascended masters and avatars so that souls could attain that ultimate union with God.

Thus, in heaven are many cosmic beings who have become such, for they have long ago taken their ascension. Though they have tarried with earth to work with those who did not make it, yet they have gone on in service at inner levels, establishing vast causal bodies of Light. Hence they are called cosmic beings, incarnations of God and of many of God's qualities.

You yourselves, beloved, have experienced at one time or another such a juxtaposition of forces of Light and Darkness—therefore my offering to you in this hour to take you to record rooms [where there is recorded] that which transpired in the Motherland that you might review your own experiences and a history that tells of the traditions of the forces sinister who have used their various ploys and plots in this century and the next, in this millennium or another. [It is our intent that] you may be able to bring to your outer mind a knowledge of these records and of what can, *what must* be done in this hour.

I come now with the fierceness of the Great Mother Kali. And that fierceness is the intensity of the white fire, which I direct to the students of the ascended masters worldwide that you might know the cutting edge of the flame and its ability as the surgeon's implement to cut away that darkness, that density, to infill and infire you and bring you to the point of the zeal of the heart, the zeal of the mind, the zeal of the desires to so manifest a vortex of flame as to rekindle many souls for Mother Mary, for Saint Germain.

Yes, beloved, I am never very far from your Mother of the Flame, from this family and the larger family of Keepers of the Flame. For I still remain Regent Mother of the Flame and I fulfill this office to the world's children, to the unborn, to souls coming into life. Thus my vigil is not only to nourish health and wisdom but to acquaint each one with the perspective of Light and Darkness and the goings on in the earth as well as the persecution of our Church, our messenger, and our chelas.

Endure, beloved, for your endurance shall surely receive the crown of everlasting life[16] and your endurance shall see judgment descend in many quarters as you keep the Flame and do not allow it to be diluted.

Do not be moved by world condemnation or any condemnation directed personally against you or the messenger; for, beloved, the condemnation of the world has been known by every aspirant after ascension's flame. I myself have known it and I myself took the words of our Lord Jesus, truly our living Saviour, "What is that to thee? Follow thou me."[17]

May the rose of the heart with an infinite number of golden pink petals unfold in you daily the joy—truly the joy of the LORD, even as the psalm of David does declare it: "The LORD is my shepherd; I shall not want. He maketh me to lie down in green pastures."[18]

Thus, beloved, beside the still waters, in the wilderness, wherever you are, our God does manifest to you. The LORD does prepare a table before you in the presence of enemies. It is the altar where there is the coming and the going of angels ascending and descending, where you receive the bliss of God and the cup of Light that runneth over, even the extension to you of the elixir of ascension's flame.

Weary not but rejoice! Lighten the karmic load by less chatter and more violet fire.

When I was in my final embodiment I had many hours to pray and I developed an intense white fire to direct into problems at a world level, those involving children and individuals for whom I would pray. That momentum came with many years of fierce, undivided attention for hours of [keeping my] morning vigil on behalf of the babies and youth.

I see so many among you for whom I did pray in this my final incarnation, and I would tell you that it is clear in the record that my prayers did make the difference in your entering the Path.

I am grateful for this but I tell it to you so that you can understand that I who have been with you so very recently in this century was able to develop that prayer momentum and therefore you can do the same. It simply takes a dedication of time and space and a determination that puts down every other voice seeking attention, every point of chaos or confusion or disruption.

When your heart and mind are stayed upon God, it creates a strong cord of living flame. Once you experience it and know how much can flow over this cord and through your crystal cord and reach many, once you know its power, yea, its omnipotence, you will not be able to turn to the right or the left; for the flame on the altar of your heart and your meditation room will be such a pull, such a blessing and surely the means to save many—not the least of whom, your own soul.

Now I invite you to take your rest, to call to the seraphim to take you to the record rooms of ancient Lemuria where you may review the scenes of ancient battles and lessons you once learned that must be reviewed. This opportunity is given in connection with the dispensations stated in the dictations of Saint Germain and Omri-Tas.[19] It is an assist that you might fulfill their calling and also take practical steps in action in the physical plane to bring about peace on earth the scientific way.

I AM the ascended lady master Clara Louise. I come to you also in the piercing flame of Mighty Victory. How I did call to him and how he did return to me Victory's fires, fire for fire as I did offer to him my daily victories!

O the ascension process! How I extol it and the God who does deliver it! May you know the beauty of the spinal altar and the stalk. May you become the most beautiful lily in the garden of God on your ascension day.

Always with you, I AM Clara Louise. Call to me, for my fire has multiplied and been multiplied by God's fire many ten thousands times ten thousands. I would give it to you. Call to our twin flames and see how we will bring our special presence and gift to the altar of this Church and the altar of your heart.

In the sweet remembrance of our oneness on ancient Lemuria, in this century, and in the worlds to come, I am surely with you always.

Seattle, Washington
May 4, 1991
10:54 P.M. P.D.T.

Self-Discipline on the Path to the Ascension

The one who shall abide in the day of the coming of the messenger of God[20] is the initiate who is self-disciplined on the path of the ascension.

Let me hasten to tell you that self-discipline is never rigid nor is it unlawfully proud. It is not accomplished at all by the carnal mind. It is the discipline of the disciple who has first loved, who has placed his head on the breast of Jesus,[21] who has known the heartbeat of the Lord and that tenderness which the human heart can scarcely contain.

Yes, beloved, true self-discipline is never rigidity but it is Love fulfilling itself by the intuitive powers of the soul, by the discrimination of the heart, by true discernment of the mind. These are inner qualities of the five secret rays that sensitize even the soul to the understanding that though all the rules be followed, yet without Love the disciple cannot succeed.

At the Ascension Temple we find that certain neophytes who are in fear of God instead of in love with God always seek to confine God to a set of rules whereby if they follow those rules, they cannot be denied. Then one day for the class at Luxor all the rules are dropped as though there were no more foundations or pillars in the temple.

Those who have sought to attain by a set of rules, beloved,

may at this point suffer temporary insanity or a prolonged lapse of sense of identity. They pale into a fear that is perhaps beyond any fear they have known. All of a sudden they have no moorings, no coordinates. They are as blind men and sense themselves so.

"How shall we fulfill the requirements of the law of Serapis," they complain, "if there be no guidelines?" To which the mentor responds: "It is by the internalization of the flame of Love that right action ensues in the Guru-chela relationship."

Therefore, if you have not internalized the Word, the Word incarnate in Jesus Christ, by assimilating his Light essence, his Body and his Blood, then the inner standard will not be developed and you can be taken only to that level where there are yet maps and rules that you can lean upon. This is good exercise, beloved, but never true attainment.

Thus, go within. Hear the call of Archangel Michael to seek adeptship[22] and do so. Love on this path is truly a disciplined love.

What is disciplined love?

It is that which moves the pen or the paintbrush, that which designs cathedrals, lays foundations for underwater passageways, mighty ships that sail the seven seas and those that journey beyond the stars. Disciplined love is the foundation of all creativity and accomplishment of design and geometry that sets the pattern of all living.

Undisciplined love is no love at all. Those who prate about love and yet do not know how to hold the strings of love taut or to tune their violins or lutes or harps, these, then, have an incomplete concept of love, which mirrors relativity but not the Absolute.

Pure and simple, absolute Love is God in complete manifestation. Relative love is but a turning around of that love to suit the human convenience of being able to talk about love. It is a

Self-Discipline on the Path to the Ascension

love that is not from the sacred altars of God but is still the human comprehension of love—of getting, forgiving, seeking recompense, seeking possession or control or favor. These perversions of love are rated as love by many, even as sympathy is sought and expressed as though it were God's love.

The charity and compassion of God sees beyond the centuries, lays foundations, prepares for future generations embodying, knows the whole circle of God's love and where a race must be in a thousand years and will work to see to it that when they arrive at the place, the place will be prepared.

Love is vision. Love is foresight. Love is taking care of details that none other will and therefore the mission should otherwise be lost.

Love is understanding the complexity of the team of lightbearers of an entire cosmos. Imagine this team, of which you are a part. Imagine how the team members have become players on this team. Imagine how they have disciplined self to take care of the details of life that have enabled another to fulfill the divine plan.

Think of a Nada, a Rose of Light, a Lady Master Venus, a Chamuel and Charity. Think of a cosmos of beings of Love and the true love your soul longs to be the recipient of—a love that truly loves the real and forgives the unreal but compels the unreal to rise and rise again and again and again until that rising is perfected in the Sun behind the sun.

O beloved, the path of the fourth ray, which we bring you this night, is a white fire that is so intense that you may not detect the golden pink glow-ray of its aura or the depths of the rose and the ruby within its stalk. Yes, beloved, love comes in all disguises of all the rays yet love is perfected in the white fire of discipleship unto the true self-discipline of the joyous ones.

Seraphim of God have come this night. They come to this city to restore the souls of many who have lost the way for centuries.

They have been called by El Morya and the Darjeeling Council. They have come for an infusion of white light that begets all Love excelling and excelling.

Many are called to the love feast. Many come at inner levels. May you call for them to be cut free by the seraphim this night to find the living reality of the path of Love embodied in the true teachings of Jesus Christ that have been lost. Yes, beloved, many on inner planes cry out to you to call to the angels to cut them free that they might make the same connection to the fount of living Love that you have made.

Love is a continuity of being.

What else could sustain you lifetime after lifetime in the imperfected state, separated and apart from your Lord as you are, having lost the hold and lost the bonding and seeking it again?

What could sustain you through the ravages of hell and the astral plane between embodiments? What could sustain your opportunity to live to love again except Love itself?

Love is impersonal yet personal. As Saint Germain has said, God is an Impersonal Impersonality, an Impersonal Personality, a Personal Personality and a Personal Impersonality. When you have figured this out on the arms of the Maltese cross, beloved, come and tell me.[23] These are the definitions of God as Father and as Son and as Mother and as Holy Spirit.

O the light rays that pierce, that pierce the dawn of earth while coming from the Central Sun! Your eyes can scarcely open to behold such light and yet you know it at inner levels. You know its secret.

You have journeyed far, yet the call of the homing has been from the heart of earth. You have known you must come. And you who are here, one and all, share a common cup of Love. You have desired to return to give, oh, so much more love than you allowed yourself to give or God to give through you in recent and ancient incarnations. You have regretted profoundly this withholding.

Now you see, now you know, now you understand that as you love all whom you meet, you will resolve and fulfill, dissolve and consign in and unto the flame all lesser manifestations. Love shall be unto you, if you claim her this night, the victory of your soul in this life.

There are others who have a dire need for Truth, for they dwell not in the Truth but in the Lie. There are others who have a need for honor, for they have been dishonorable toward life. But the need of all here, and the desiring, is to be in that flame of Love and to give it. This is what is the common note and the communality of all of you and of all upon earth who share the ascended masters' teachings.

For what is this teaching but the Divine Love of God, who has come to nurture your soul and answer her questions and give the Divine Doctrine?

The love you have received must beget great God-gratitude. Thus, in giving again and again, you, my beloved, shall reach for and pick that rose of light that comes from the heart of the Divine Mother.

In the bliss of God, I AM Clara Louise. Know that there is no true Divine Love without pain, for the pain is what true Divine Love flushes out. Fear not to touch upon and to experience ancient and recent pains—and let them pass, let them pass into the flame, into the river Ganges, into the hearts of saints and back to God.

Yes, beloved, let there no longer be the suppression, let there no longer be the placing of the wall around yourself to insulate yourself from pain. Pain approaches the edge of bliss then dissolves into it. This is the knowing of true love.

I wish you, with all of my heart and my prayers, the fulfilling of the mystery of Love in this life. The mystery is elusive. It plays hide-and-seek with you.

The more love you carry, beloved, the more it shall cause the hatred to come out in others. You say, "How can this be true love?" True love is a purging fire. If you decide to carry it to such an intensity, you shall become the Refiner's fire.

Do not hold back your will from entering in to this experience, for many are the prisoners of their own hatreds of centuries. They cannot get away from them. They are in bondage. They cannot escape. It requires the surgery of love and the holding of that one until love does consume that wall of hatred.

If you fear to be bruised and beaten by those to whom you give love, then you are not yet ready to carry the Saviour's love. Begin with little loves, for they are seeds planted and they become beautiful unfolding flowers that grow and grow. You shall be strengthened in this process and you shall know little by little the gratitude that comes from those who could not have been saved unless you had embodied that flaming fire.

Many, many, beloved, are bound by the karma of Love's perversions. Will you not be the representatives of angels and ascended masters of the third ray of love and of the Holy Spirit itself to speak to these ones, to minister to them?

Realize also that it is sometimes best that you remain anonymous, praying fervently and fasting even on behalf of those whom you know not, that they might receive that love and be liberated.

Contemplate, then, how great must be that love to liberate a single soul from the grips of Death and Hell. Truly the astral plane is a place where people are "brainwashed," as they say. Their minds are controlled to believe that that which is offered to them by fallen angels is in their best interest. To tear them from this and to give them the gift of beginning life over again under the true Divine Parents, this is the mighty, mighty work of Love!

Know that it awaits you when you are ready.

And if you are just beginning this path, take up, then, Love's own violet ray and flame and the purple fire and use it, beloved. Use it, I say, to purge yourself of love that is unreal and to fill yourself with love that is real.

I am your friend on the path of Love. If you call to me, I will give you a recounting of many, many incidents in my life in which I devised the means of self-discipline whereby I did conserve the sacred fire of Love and therefore had the power, mighty indeed, to convey it to others who had nothing at all in the cups of their chakras.

Know this joy of being Divine Love in action to supply the love that only God can give and that you have stored in your cups. Give to those who are able to take of the cup of living Love and not dash it. Retain and hold the balance for others who would only lose it, to their loss and yours.

Therefore be wise and let the All-Seeing Eye of God at the point of the brow become for you a point of single-minded, true discernment and discrimination in order that compassion may flow where compassion does compel.

I seal you in the ruby cross and the flame of the Ruby Buddha, who shall salute you in this conference.

New Orleans, Louisiana
October 12, 1991
1:43 A.M. C.D.T.

The Honor of God

My beloved children, I address you one and all as my children. For I have nourished you, I have prayed for you in the many decades preceding my ascension after I had learned the power of decrees.

I consider all the people of the world my children but most especially do I honor those who keep the cosmic honor flame, those who understand that the honor of God is all. And if we cannot keep the honor of God, then all other virtues tumble—tumble like play blocks in a child's nursery.

The honor of God is to be espoused. When you walk this path of honor, you see your Holy Christ Self by and by. The Holy Christ Self will allow you to see the honor of God manifest within him, that you might mirror that great honor that God accords to all life—all life ascending, all life tending to the realities, to what is important.

Blessed ones, I made it my devotion to begin as early as four in the morning and sometimes three, giving my calls specifically for the youth of the world of all ages. In the latter years as in the earlier years, I would spend four to five to six hours every morning doing nothing else until I had made every last call to the Keeper of the Scrolls, to the Lords of Karma on behalf of the children. I would call to Archangel Michael and especially to

The Honor of God

Mother Mary.

The messenger has had in her files records of my writing between the lines of the Keepers of the Flame Lessons as I have pondered those lessons and used them paragraph by paragraph to form my invocations and my prayers. I was determined that every opportunity, every lesson, every command that was given by the Knight Commander—that I would fulfill that request, I would fulfill whatever it might be that God called upon us to do through the *Pearls of Wisdom,* through the dictations and through those lessons. How I have been enriched, beloved! How I have been enriched!

The messenger will speak to you concerning your sacred labor in life.[24] Ponder the meaning of the sacred labor, beloved, for it is all-important. You must have a sacred labor if you are to achieve immortality. And you must be ready at all times to lay that labor upon the altar of God and enter the Sacred Heart of our Lord and Saviour Jesus Christ.

So I come to you, beloved. So I come and place my Presence now over the beloved messenger. I, then, send to you from my heart and her heart, we as one—I, the messenger above, she the messenger below—thus we give you the flame of the honor of God. May you keep that honor and may your honor become transparent. May you become the transparency for the honor of God. When you look into the eyes of souls of such purity and you see that, beloved, you know that you have walked in the footsteps of the saints.

Now, beloved, I touch you each one in a touch of comfort and consolation. In this world there is travail, there is sorrow, but as it is said, "joy cometh in the morning."[25] What is the morning but the dawn of your eternal reality! Every day the sun crests the mountains and you behold again the victory of our God, the legions of angels crisscrossing the worlds in all dimensions and all levels of being. Oh, what a joy it is to travel with the angels of the dawn! Perhaps Archangel Uriel shall invite you to travel with these angels. And as you go, you never go into the darkness, for you are always following the dawn.

I, then, desire you to know that I am your Mother, your sister at your side. Call to me, for when you call to me for anything, I receive an empowerment from you. You know the law that I cannot act in your behalf unless you give me that energy, give me that call. Blessed ones, sometimes I wonder if anyone will knock upon my door at Luxor. Therefore I hope and trust that I shall not have to wonder anymore. So when the first rays of the dawn greet you in the morning, remember to send me your heart's love so that I might multiply your gift to me and send you forth intensifying, intensifying, intensifying the sweetness of God's love.

I seal you, then. I have been with you from the Beginning. And I will be there, wherever you are, in the hour of your ascension. I promise you: *I shall be there.*

In the light of Elohim, may you prosper and prosper unto the glory of your soul.

Royal Teton Ranch
Park County, Montana
October 13, 1996
3:15 P.M. M.D.T.

CHAPTER 15

Remembrances of Those Who Knew Her

I Loved Her Then and I Love Her Now

It was about the year 1938 that I came to know beloved Louise Kieninger. We were both students of Saint Germain's activity under the messengership of the Ballards, in the New York City sanctuary. Miss Kieninger was an aristocratic, beautifully dressed woman with a serene countenance and a deeply spiritual quality which exuded from her entire being.

I barely knew her until I was called upon to accept the leadership of the New York sanctuary and I invited her, as a devoted student, to take the leadership of the violet-flame class. At that time a very strong bond of friendship grew between us. It became quite obvious that there were some old attachments or close relationships between us from some distant past. Within a few months' time, Louise gave up her New York residency as well as her position with the Red Cross, and she moved to Scarsdale to reside with me. We had become inseparable, and my husband and family accepted her as a part of the family also. Many were the wonderful times we all had together. Multitudinous are the wonderful memories of those happy days.

The secret of our happiness together lay in our mutual respect of one another's privacy and our deep devotion to our common love, the light and illumination of the masters. Nothing had ever come between us. Miss Louise was always willing to accept whatever plans were made without any intrusion of her own opinions or desire—a saintly quality with which few on earth are endowed.

Miss Louise had a tremendous talent for organization. That was her greatest service to life. She was happiest when there was some form of organization to be accomplished. She was strict in her ethics regarding any organization to which she gave her endeavors. Any deviation gave her much concern, though she would never admit to being anything but serene in the face of all problems. Often she would say, "What is that to me!" or "Consider the source." I can hear her now as she so often brought to mind the master's words "What is that to thee? Follow thou me!" She lived that thought continuously. I remember her in my heart repeating those words again and again and again when there was a need.

It is my tribute to her to remember her undeviating honesty and love, her faith in the masters, and her steadfast endeavor to tread the narrow way, undeterred by anyone or any other thought, feeling, or desire. I loved her then. I love her now. I revere her memory as I revered her as a person. We lived so joyously together for so long, and in truth our hearts have never been separated. I know that we shall work together again, as even now I feel her Presence and her influence and her love around me.

Mary Myneta Boos
(Mrs. Sterling F. Boos)
Scarsdale, New York
September 21, 1974

Sessions of Sweet Silent Thought

When to the sessions of sweet silent thought
I summon up remembrance of things past,
I sigh the lack of many a thing I sought,
And with old woes new wail my dear times' waste:
. . . . .
But if the while I think on thee, dear friend,
All losses are restor'd and sorrows end.
William Shakespeare

    The dear, beautiful face swam through a blur of my tears as she turned once more and waved to me. I was in the Union Station in Denver and she was seeing me off. I was all of eighteen years old, and for the past month had been a guest of Clara Louise Kieninger at the Nurses' Home of Colorado General Hospital, where she was Director of the School of Nursing. I felt that I could not bear the parting. But I would not cry. For one of the things I had learned in the past month was that there is always a new beginning, the future is full of adventure and is what we make it, that our fate is in our hands, and that nothing beautiful or worthwhile is ever lost, which also included this new, wonderful friendship.

    That was the first of my many visits to Denver.

One could say that my relationship with Louise Kieninger started even before I was born. My father's eldest brother and his family lived as a neighbor to the Kieningers, and my father was a frequent visitor to his brother's home and also to the Kieningers' home. Both families were members of the same church, and my uncle's sister-in-law married Louise's eldest brother. Also, her other brother Will and my father became best friends. Time went by, my father married my mother, my uncle moved, and other changes were wrought, but the families remained close friends.

I was nine years old when the armistice ending the First World War was signed. It meant little to me except that the war which had been going on ever since I could remember was now ended. But soon there was talk among friends and relatives that Louise Kieninger was coming home. This was a name I had heard many times: "A letter came from Louise"; "Louise is now in England"; "Louise is leaving London"; "Louise is now in France"; "Louise is at the front." Now she was coming home.

In her memoirs she recounts her appointment as Superintendent of Nurses at Christ Hospital in Topeka after her return from the war. I remember one meeting with her in 1919 or 1920. One Sunday afternoon my mother and aunt went to call on her at Christ Hospital and took me with them. My memory is of tree-shaded grounds and a dim room where leafy light filtered through the windows. The walls were book-lined. A gracious lady sat there talking to my aunt and mother, asked me a few questions, and learned from my mother that I was taking piano lessons and was doing quite well.

It was during this period that my piano teacher presented me in a recital of my own at a local church. Louise sent a huge basket of flowers. I was *so* impressed that the Superintendent of Nurses at Christ Hospital would send me flowers. This was typical of her thoughtfulness and encouragement.

As I write this, it occurs to me to wonder why there was not more contact with her during this two years that she was in Topeka. I think the answer must be that she was more a friend to my father's family than my mother's, and she and my mother were not particularly close.

Then off she went to Brazil. Again, glamour and mystery of faraway places surrounded her name.

When Louise returned from Brazil in 1926, I was in junior high school. She and her sister Cecelia (for whom I was named) came to our house for Sunday dinner. I had been brought up in a strictly "children should be seen and not heard" sort of family, so when Louise drew me into the conversation, asked about my school courses, my desires and ambitions, and then asked me to play for her, it was like the opening of a door with sunshine pouring in. As she left, she said, "When you finish high school, I want you to come to Denver and stay with me for a while." I felt as if all the fairy stories I had ever read were coming true for me; a fairy godmother was waving her wand over me, and I felt as if I might become a princess any moment!

In the summer of 1927, after graduation from high school, I went for my first visit to Denver. Louise had come to Topeka to visit her family and took me back with her. With what awe I looked at her as we sat opposite each other in the Pullman; I was almost afraid to touch her for fear she would vanish and it would all be a dream. This may sound unduly naïve for a high-school graduate of eighteen, but sophistication came more slowly in those days. I had been an only child, brought up by strict "spare the rod and spoil the child" parents. I knew I was loved. I was well provided for, I had nice clothes, I was given music lessons; but my parents, aunts and uncles felt it necessary to preserve a certain distance from their children in order to avoid spoiling them. Louise was a being from another world who had singled me out for her attention. I felt as if I had been kissed by an angel.

She took me to her rooms in the Nurses' Home at the

hospital. I had a room of my own for sleeping, but spent my waking hours in her suite browsing through her books, or at the piano in the basement, practicing. I could not practice in the nurses' living room, because the night nurses were sleeping during the day. In the evenings, though, I could play in the living room, and I did this often. Louise's frequent request was for Liszt's "Liebestraum" no. 3, which I played as written with all the cadenzas. The evening always ended with this selection. It remained a favorite of hers throughout her life, and she requested it for her ascension service.

Later we would sit on her balcony looking at the stars and talking about the universe and about God. She taught me that God is Love, and that by right thinking we put ourselves in harmony with God. Negative thoughts bring negative results; we are what we think. These ideas were revolutionary to me, who had been brought up in a strictly fundamentalist atmosphere.

Two books of hers that made a deep impression on me at that time were *Life and Teachings of the Masters of the Far East* by Baird T. Spalding and *The Prophet* by Kahlil Gibran. Regarding the book on the masters, I said, "Do you really think that's true?" She replied, "Well, it *could* be, couldn't it?" I said yes, I guess it could. And that book was the first introduction to the masters.

One day, struggling with my unruly hair, which was cut in a short bob, I said in exasperation, "Oh, it just *won't* behave!" She said, "Won't?" I said, "No, it just won't." "Of course it won't when you say so," she replied. "Don't you see that you are making a law for it when you declare it won't behave?" Lesson No. 1.

Another time we were taking a walk in the early evening. I, at the ripe age of eighteen, aware that she had put in a long day's work and also aware that she was in her "near-senile forties," was holding her arm and helping her up and down the curbs. She pulled free and said, "Don't do that." I said, "Aren't you tired?" She turned to me and the blue eyes flashed. "Don't *ever* ask me if I'm tired! I'm *never* tired. There is always energy all around me for the taking; all I have to do is reach out and accept it." Lesson No. 2.

There were many more lessons. Every day something would occur that would bring home her lessons in constructive thinking, in positiveness, kindliness to others.

Another time, by an indiscreet, thoughtless remark, I had caused a mild misunderstanding. Fearing that I had displeased her, I sat and moped throughout the evening. "Why are you sad?" she asked. "I'm sorry for what I said to Mrs. ———; I can't bear to offend you." She looked straight at me. "Cecilia, you can't offend me. I'm never offended by what other people say or do. I rise above such personalities."

Because of my upbringing, I was always quiet in the presence of my elders. On one of our evening walks, she asked, "What are you thinking?" "Oh, I was just thinking how good the air smells and how glad I am to be here." "Then you should say so. You must do your part in keeping conversation going when you are with others. You owe that much to your hostess." Another pointer along the road to poise and maturity.

That summer was a time of indecisiveness for me as far as my own future was concerned. I had received a scholarship for piano study in one of the prominent conservatories in the Middle West, but the scholarship would not pay all the expenses and I knew my parents could give me no help. I could give up the scholarship, go to business college and prepare for an office position, or borrow the money for the conservatory. Or try to work my way through. It was Louise who gave me the courage to go on with what I wanted. She asked, "What do you want to do?"

"Well, I'd like to use my scholarship and study music."

"Then that's the thing for you to do."

"But I don't know if I can. My folks won't want me to go away from home. I won't have the courage to defy them if they forbid it."

"If that's what you want, then tell them in a firm but gentle way that that is your decision. A way will be opened. You must have the courage to do what your heart tells you is right for you. Hold your head up and know that whatever comes, you will be able to face it."

Many times those words came back to me. I *did* go to the conservatory, I *did* get a part-time job, and I *did* borrow the money. My years at that college were among the happiest of my life, and I earned my bachelor's degree in two years and a summer session. Later, when a depression had the entire country in its grip and people had little money for food, much less for music study, discouragement and even despair came upon me. Always there was the echo from that summer: "Know that whatever comes, you will be able to face it." I did go to a business college and took office positions thereafter; but by that time I had my degree and my musical skill, and it has been a source of joy and comfort to me and, I hope, to others.

I still see her as she was then: the way she moved; her erect, queenly carriage which she retained to the end of her earthly life; the naturally curly, slightly graying hair that needed only to be brushed back simply and pinned in a chignon; the gracious smile; the stern flash of blue eyes when the occasion warranted it. I loved the scent that was so much a part of her. The packages and letters I later received from her were permeated with it. Oh, I knew the labels on the bottles and powder boxes in her room, but those perfumes and powders never smelled the same on me or anyone else. It was a fragrance that emanated from *her*.

I loved, when coming in late at night, going with her through the dimly lighted hospital corridors, visiting patients on the critical list, post-operatives, or others that needed a touch of the hand here, an encouraging word there. There would be a question to this nurse, some instruction to another. Louise was personally involved with all of her patients and all of her nurses.

So when I stood in the Union Station in Denver and waved goodbye to her, I felt some magic was going out of my life. I wanted to stay with her forever, as Peter, James and John wanted to build tabernacles and stay permanently on the mountaintop where Jesus was transfigured. But there was work to be done; they had to descend from the mountaintop, and I had to go to college. So I blinked back the tears and knew that "whatever comes, you will be able to face it."

Later visits to her in Denver were much the same. They are etched in my memory as sunlit intervals throughout the years. I took my problems, my fears, my dreams, and my joys to her. At different times she introduced me to her friends and colleagues. One summer she took me to meet Robert Schmitz, the great French pianist, during the time he was conducting a master class in Denver. Another year it was Rudolph Ganz, with whom I later earned a scholarship at the Chicago Musical College.

Our paths divided again. In 1941 she gave up her position in Denver and, with the threat of war, was again sent to Brazil by the Rockefeller Foundation to assist in setting up their defense program. Meanwhile, I was working, playing, living quite a prosaic life at home. War broke out in Europe, then came Pearl Harbor, and we were in the conflict.

I had married and was living in Washington, D.C., when Louise returned from Brazil and I saw her again. Then she went east to New York and we came west to California. Letters, phone calls, a few meetings when she was in charge of the Saint Germain Youth Camp at Mount Shasta.

In 1958 my husband, fourteen-year-old daughter, and I drove to New York, and we saw Louise again. She was living in the house on East Seventy-second Street, where she had initiated the Mother of the Flame Activity. The sanctuary in that house was beautiful, all in violet. I had the privilege of playing the organ there. Again I played "Liebestraum" for her. As we were leaving and I was hugging her, I was somewhat startled by her frailness, and for the first time it occurred to me: "She is mortal. One of these days she will be leaving us." Nevertheless, she continued her activities and never gave an inkling that she was less strong and vigorous than she had been.

Louise came to live with us in March of 1968, and thus our association came full circle. Her frailty now was a fact with which we had to deal, but never an admission from her. We sought medical advice; she was put on a diet of whole grains and legumes that only aggravated her ailment and caused her great suffering. Between us, we finally hit on a diet of milk, eggs, and puréed vegetables that nourished her and caused no distress. She had not eaten meat for many years.

Every day she rose, had her breakfast, then went immediately to her room and had her Mother of the Flame Service. In spite of pain in her back and neck, she spent long hours at her table writing her memoirs. Finally the memoirs were finished. She said: "I have fulfilled El Morya's request; the book is finished. Now I can go home."

Gradually she became feebler, spent more hours resting in her bed, and finally one morning could not rise, could not speak to me. She was taken to a local hospital where they instituted measures to prolong her life. I went every day to see her; and she would struggle with the intravenous tubes that were pouring nourishment into her, and say to me: "Why don't they leave me alone? I don't want to get well; I want to go home." I knew what she meant; she did not mean home to my house. She always knew that beloved Serapis Bey and her Twin Flame would meet her when she was ready to go. A few days later, on October 25,

1970, she went Home.
   Auf Wiedersehen, Louise!

> Cecilia Senne Lewis
> Berkeley, California
> September 22, 1974

The Sacred Labor

Reflecting on the memoirs of Clara Louise, I cannot help but add one word for those who have also found inspiration in her life. For to me her life epitomized what El Morya refers to as the *sacred labor*. The concept of the sacred labor has become nearer and dearer to my heart as I have contemplated the community of the Holy Spirit that has been the dream of El Morya for his chelas as a means to both personal and planetary evolution.

Taken from the archetype of the City Foursquare that rises from the foundation of self-mastery in the four lower bodies, the community of the Holy Spirit is the group effort of souls united in the sacred labor. When we contemplate the life of Jesus, we find that his practical Christianity, his path of working the works of God in man, began in a humble home where, tutored by his mother in the things of the spirit, he was at an early age apprenticed to his father to learn the trade of the carpenter.

In the Essene community at Qumran, an example of the community of the Holy Spirit, each man's sacred labor was held in reverence by all. Each man and woman, as an initiate of the Christ, was required to gain mastery in the planes of Matter by fulfilling the mandates of a particular calling, trade or profession. This became not only his contribution to the community, but also the means for the perfectionment of his soul. Thus in every age the sacred labor provides the means whereby the soul can balance the threefold flame and pass the tests of the seven rays in practice as well as in theory.

At Summit University in Santa Barbara, California, students of the ascended masters attend a series of five 12-week seminars in which they learn the precepts of the law, practice meditation and the science of invocation, learn the art of prayer and fasting, and come to grips with cycles of past karma while studying methods of transmutation through the application of the sacred fire. During alternate co-op periods, students are required to work in the world community, to hold jobs, and to learn the responsibility of service as they perfect their sacred labor.

They are taught to strive for perfection in every aspect of life as a means to creative fulfillment and to the mastery of the energies of the soul. They are encouraged to take jobs which will enable them to discover that certain genius which God has given to everyone. They must determine, if they have not already done so, what their life's calling is and how they can best respond to the requirements of the soul's blueprint for life while keeping the vows they took before the Lords of Karma prior to this embodiment.

As they advance in their studies, students give thought as to what their sacred labor will be, what supreme service is theirs to perfect and to offer to the individual, to the upliftment of the race, and to society as a whole. Whether a trade or a profession, with or without monetary reward, the sacred labor—as the talent that is multiplied, the tool that is sharpened—is the means whereby the student establishes his soul's worth both to himself and to his fellowman. The sacred labor as the inner calling of the soul must be perfected in a practical mode that has application in the day-to-day needs of the community. The sacred labor is an indispensable component of the path of self-realization. It is the implementation of the Flame of the Holy Spirit.

By the sacred labor, men and women realize their potential to be the Christ in action as well as in contemplation. Through the sacred labor, students perfect certain skills necessary to the mastery of an aspect of time and space, that they might ultimately learn the mastery of self. Trained in the things of the Spirit, students of Summit University go forth to lead balanced lives (whether they marry and raise families or remain celibate) and become responsible members of the world community. Thus they are able to relate to the now of earthly existence, to the needs of family, friends, and neighbors, all the while pursuing the goal of the ascension and helping others to follow the true teachings of Christ as defined by the ascended masters.

The life of Clara Louise Kieninger is of special importance to those who look to her guru, Serapis Bey, as the Hierarch of the Ascension Temple and as the teacher whose discipline they require in order to become candidates for the ascension. Keepers of the Flame who read her vivid recollections (which she did not write down till she was in her eighties) will realize that her ascension was earned by the grace of God through faith and through works.

Long before Clara Louise ever encountered the hierarchy of ascended masters, her life was dedicated to the discipline and the service of the Lord. Truly a life lived in Christ, having as its theme the sacred labor, is one that has merit both on earth and in heaven. The crowning glory of her service was, of course, the vigil she held for the youth of the world and the fiery and almost fierce decree momentum which she developed over many years.

All of this was possible because the foundation of self-discipline and selfless service had already been laid. It was a natural transition from a direct and personal service to a limited number of people to an indirect and impersonal ritual of prayer and invocation on behalf of all.

There comes a time in the evolution of the soul when work without the inspiration of a goal beyond the self no longer has meaning. We say to ourselves that if we are to continue, we must dedicate our work to the glory of God and to the service of our fellowman. Only by so doing can we know true joy. It is at that moment that our work becomes the sacred labor.

As we seek the perfect integration of Spirit in Matter and of Matter in Spirit, Clara Louise, by her flame and by her excellence, shows us what one life lived one-pointedly can achieve on a person-to-person basis and how the sacred labor can culminate in a world-wide expansion of the Mother flame on behalf of all mankind. Let all who aspire to the ascension realize that until our work becomes our sacred labor and until our faith has practical application in our work, our life record, when reviewed before the Lords of Karma, will be found wanting.

Let all then consider the sacred labor as an essential part of the path to reunion with God. Let all pray for the energy and the divine direction as well as the vision that will enable them to apply themselves in the world with the greatest efficiency and the greatest effectivity in Love for the progress of the individual and of civilization as a whole.

The life of Clara Louise Kieninger was in its totality a sacred labor that culminated in the ascension of her soul to the level of the I AM Presence. In her sacred labor, she left a mark of perfection in the nursing profession which will forever be a momentum of power, wisdom and love to all who come after her. This, then, is our highest responsibility: to use the sacred labor as a means of leaving footprints in the sands of time which clearly mark the way of perfection for those who are following the Christ in the regeneration.

Elizabeth Clare Prophet
The Motherhouse
Santa Barbara, California
September 14, 1974

Notes

Chapter 12

1. Saint Germain to "Friends of Freedom," March 7, 1961.
2. El Morya to "Chelas of God's Own Will," January 31, 1961.
3. Ibid.
4. Casimir Poseidon, September 12, 1965.
5. *Summit Beacon,* December 1965.
6. Matt. 26:40–41.
7. John 14:12.
8. *"Watch With Me": Jesus' Vigil of the Hours* (Corwin Springs, Mont.: The Summit Lighthouse, 1987), pp. 3–4.
9. Emma Lazarus, The New Colossus: Inscription for the Statue of Liberty, New York Harbor.
10. *Liberty Proclaims* (Colorado Springs, Colo.: The Summit Lighthouse, 1967), pp. ix–x.
11. Goddess of Liberty, February 28, 1965.
12. El Morya to his chelas, May 21, 1966, Program for Freedom Class 1966.
13. Mother Mary to "Those Who Would Honor Him," February 1969, Program for Class of the Resurrection Flame, Easter 1969.

Chapter 14

1. Luke 24: 13–35.
2. Rom. 12:1.
3. Isa. 65:24.
4. II Cor. 12:7.
5. Matt. 6:33.
6. I Cor. 15:52, 54.
7. Matt. 19:26.
8. I Cor. 15:26.
9. Eph. 4:22–24; Col. 3:9–10.

10. I Cor. 15:31.
11. II Cor. 6:2.
12. See Kuthumi and Djwal Kul, *The Human Aura* (Corwin Springs, Mont.: Summit University Press, 1996), book 2, chapter 8.
13. I Cor. 9:24–27; Heb. 12:1.
14. The "Triumphal March," or "Grand March," is from the opera *Aïda*, by Giuseppe Verdi. It is song 224, "All Hail, Mighty Serapis Bey," in *Church Universal and Triumphant Book of Hymns and Songs*.
15. Ezek. 1:4.
16. James1:12; Rev. 2:10.
17. John 21:22.
18. Ps. 23.
19. See dictations by Saint Germain and Omri-Tas, May 1, 1991, "The Outline of a Maltese Cross" and "A Violet Flame Sea of Light," in *Pearls of Wisdom,* vol. 34, no. 26, June 24, 1991.
20. Mal. 3:1–3.
21. John 13:23, 25; 21:20.
22. Archangel Michael, August 11, 1991, "New Beginnings," in *Pearls of Wisdom,* vol. 34, no., 47, October 6, 1991.
23. See *Saint Germain On Alchemy* (Corwin Springs, Mont.: Summit University Press, 1993), pp. 74–75, 277–84.
24. The messenger gave teaching about the sacred labor during darshan on October 18, 1996.
25. Ps. 30:5.

Glossary

Words set in *italics* are defined elsewhere in the Glossary.

Amen Bey, the ascended master. *Twin Flame* of the ascended lady Clara Louise. Amen Bey was embodied numerous times in Egypt where he was at one time a pharaoh. He was a priest of the sacred fire on Atlantis and works closely with *Serapis Bey* in the *Ascension* Temple at Luxor.

Angel. An "angle" of God's consciousness; an aspect of his Self-awareness; an individualization of the creative fires of the *cosmos*. The angelic hosts are an evolution of beings set apart from the evolutions of mankind by their flaming selfhood and by their purity of devotion to the Godhead and to the God-free beings they serve. Their function is to concentrate, intensify, and amplify the energies of God on behalf of the entire creation. They minister to the needs of mankind by intensifying feelings of hope, faith, and charity, honor and integrity, truth and freedom, mercy and justice, and every aspect of the crystal clarity of the mind of God.

Angels are electrons revolving around the Sun Presence that is God—electrons who have elected to expand his consciousness in every plane of being. They are rods and cones of concentrated energy that can be diverted into action by the Christed ones wherever and whenever there is a need. There are angels of healing, protection, love, comfort and compassion, angels attending the cycles of life and death, angels who wield the flaming sword of truth to cleave asunder the real from the unreal. There are types and orders of angels who perform specific services in the cosmic *hierarchy*.

The fallen angels are those who followed *Lucifer* in the Great Rebellion and whose consciousness therefore "fell" to lower levels of awareness as they were by law "cast out into the earth" (Rev. 12:9) where they continue to amplify the luciferian rebellion. They are known as the fallen ones, sons of Belial, the *Luciferians*.

Angel deva. *See* Deva.

Archangel. An *angel* who has passed certain advanced initiations qualifying him to preside over lesser angels and bands of angels. Each of the *seven rays* has an archangel who, with his divine complement, an *archeia,* presides over the angels serving on that ray. The archangels and archeiai of the rays are as follows: First ray, Archangel Michael and Faith; second ray, Archangel Jophiel and Christine; third ray, Archangel Chamuel and Charity; fourth ray, Archangel Gabriel and Hope; fifth ray, Archangel Raphael and Mary; sixth ray, Archangel Uriel and Aurora; seventh ray, Archangel Zadkiel and Holy Amethyst.

Archangel Gabriel and Hope. The *archangel* and *archeia* of the fourth *ray* of the *ascension* flame. Gabriel is known as the Angel of the Annunciation. Their retreat is located on the *etheric plane* between Sacramento and Mount Shasta in California.

Archeia (*pl.* archeiai). Feminine complement of an *archangel.*

Ascended master. One who has mastered time and space and in the process gained the mastery of the self, balanced at least 51 percent of his *karma,* fulfilled his divine plan, and ascended into the Presence of the I AM THAT I AM; one who inhabits the planes of *Spirit*, or heaven.

Ascension. The ritual whereby the soul reunites with the *Spirit*, the *I AM Presence*. The ascension is the final initiation of the soul after its sojourn in time and space. It is the reward of the righteous that is the gift of God after the final judgment in which every man is judged according to his works. (Rev. 20:12) The ascension was demonstrated publicly by Elijah, who ascended "in a chariot of fire"(II Kings 2:11), and by Jesus, who ascended into the cloud of his I AM Presence from Bethany's hill (Acts 1: 8, 9). It is the goal of life for the *sons and daughters of God*.

Atlantis. The continent which existed where the Atlantic Ocean now is and which sank in cataclysm. According to James Churchward, this occurred more than 11,600 years ago (*The Lost Continent of Mu* [New York: Ives Washburn, 1931], p. 264).

Ballard, Edna. *Messenger* for the *Great White Brotherhood* from the late 1920s to the year 1971, when she made her *ascension* on February 12. Now the ascended lady master Lotus. She was embodied as Saint Joan of Arc and in her final embodiment served with her husband and *twin flame, Guy W. Ballard*, to found the I AM movement sponsored by *Saint Germain* under a dispensation of the *Great White Brotherhood*. Her pen name was Lotus Ray King.

Ballard, Guy W. *Messenger* for the *Great White Brotherhood* from the late 1920s to the year 1939, when he made his *ascension* on December 31. Now the *ascended master* Godfre, also known as God Obedience. He was embodied as Richard the Lionhearted and as George Washington. In his final embodiment, with his wife and *twin flame, Edna Ballard*, he founded the I AM movement under the direction of the ascended master *Saint Germain*. His pen name was Godfré Ray King. His most important works are *Unveiled Mysteries*, *The Magic Presence*, and *The "I AM" Discourses*.

Bodies of man. The four lower bodies are four sheaths consisting of four distinct frequencies which surround the soul—the physical, emotional, mental, and etheric. They are the modes of the soul in its journey through time and space. The three higher bodies are the *Christ Self*, the *I AM Presence*, and the *Causal Body*.

Casimir Poseidon. The *ascended master* who ruled an ancient civilization on the continent of South America during its rise through the heights of a *golden age* and during its decline, when the people rebelled against God and his laws and the ascended masters finally withdrew from contact with the masses. The motto which he gave to the people was "Learn to do well, and you shall." The figure of the Greek god Poseidon comes down to us from the memory of this majestic ruler.

Causal Body. The body of First Cause; concentric spheres of *light* and consciousness surrounding the *I AM Presence* in the planes of *Spirit*. These concentric forcefields of electronic energy are available to the soul to work the works of God upon earth. The energies of the causal body may be drawn forth through invocation in the name of the Christ to the I AM Presence. The Causal Body is the dwelling place of the Most High God to which Jesus referred when he said, "In my Father's house are many mansions." (John 14:2) The Causal Body is the mansion or the habitation of the Spirit to which the soul returns through the ritual of the *ascension*. The causal body as the star of each man's divine individuality was referred to by Paul when he said, "One star differeth from another star in glory." (I Cor. 15:41)

Chela. In India, a disciple of a religious teacher (Hindi *celā* from Sanskrit *ceta* "slave" or "servant"). A term used generally to refer to a student of the *ascended masters* and their teachings. Specifically, a student of more than ordinary self-discipline and devotion initiated by an ascended master and serving the cause of the *Great White Brotherhood*.

Chohan. Tibetan for lord or master; a chief. Each of the *seven rays* has a chohan who focuses the *Christ consciousness* of the ray. The names of the chohans of the rays are as follows: First ray, *El Morya;* second ray, Lanto; third ray, Paul the Venetian; fourth ray, *Serapis Bey;* fifth ray, Hilarion; sixth ray, Nada; seventh ray, *Saint Germain.*

Christ consciousness. The consciousness or awareness of the self as the Christ; the attainment of a level of consciousness commensurate with that which was realized by Jesus the Christ. The Christ consciousness is the fulfillment within the self of that mind which was in Christ Jesus. It is the attainment of the balanced awareness of power, wisdom, and love —of Father, Son, and Holy Spirit—through the balanced manifestation of the *threefold flame* within the heart.

Christ Self. The individualized focus of "the only begotten of the Father full of grace and truth" (John 1:14); the universal Christ individualized as the true identity of the soul; the *Real Self* of every man, woman, and child to which the soul must rise. The Christ Self is the mediator between a man and his God; it is a man's own personal mentor, priest, and prophet, master and teacher. Total identification with the Christ Self defines the Christed one, the Christed being, or the *Christ consciousness.*

Color rays. The *light* emanations of the Godhead; e.g., the seven rays of the white light which emerge through the prism of the

Christ consciousness are (1) blue, (2) yellow, (3) pink, (4) white, (5) green, (6) purple and gold, and (7) violet. There are also five "secret rays" which emerge from the white-fire core of being.

Community of the Holy Spirit. (1) The communion of souls serving the Holy Spirit who are one in love, in truth, in life, working together for the benefit of mankind and the establishment of the *golden age*. (2) An actual physical community which such souls establish to further the aims of the *Great White Brotherhood* and to fulfill individually their *sacred labor;* e.g., the Essene community in Qumran.

Cosmic being. An *ascended master* who has attained *cosmic consciousness* and ensouls the energies of many worlds and systems of worlds within this galaxy and beyond.

Cosmic consciousness. (1) God's awareness of himself in and as the *cosmos*. (2) Man's awareness of himself in and as God's cosmic self-awareness. The awareness of the self fulfilling the cycles of the cosmos; the awareness of the self as God in cosmic dimensions; the attainment of initiations leading to a cosmic awareness of selfhood.

Cosmic Virgin. The Divine Mother, specifically in her awareness of the *cosmic consciousness* of wholeness.

Cosmos. The world or universe regarded as an orderly, harmonious system. The material cosmos consists of the entire manifestation in the planes of *Matter* of universes known and unknown. All that exists in time and space comprises the cosmos. There is also a spiritual cosmos, which includes the counterpart of the material cosmos and beyond.

Cyclopea. *Elohim* of the Fifth *Ray* (the ray of science, healing, and truth). Known as the Great Silent Watcher, the All-

Seeing Eye of God, and the Elohim of Music. Cyclopea represents the fifth ray on the Karmic Board.

Darjeeling Council. A council of the *Great White Brotherhood* headed by the *ascended master El Morya,* its chief. The Darjeeling Council trains souls in the laws of God and man and serves to implement the will of God and God-government upon earth. The council meets in the Temple of God's Will on the etheric plane over Darjeeling, India.

Deathless solar body. The seamless garment (John 19:23); the wedding garment (Matt. 22:12); the forcefield of *light* woven by the soul as an energy matrix which the soul uses to make the transition from the planes of *Matter* to the planes of *Spirit.*

Decree. (1) *n.* (a) a foreordaining will, an edict or fiat, a foreordaining of events; (b) a prayer invoking the *light* of God for and on behalf of the evolutions of mankind in the name of the Christ and in the name of the *I AM Presence.* (2) *v.* (a) to decide, to declare, to command or enjoin; to determine or order; to ordain; (b) to invoke the light of God aloud by the power of the spoken word in rhythm and in harmony.

The decree is the most powerful of all applications to the Godhead. It is the command of the *son or daughter of God* made in the name of the I AM Presence and the Christ for the will of the Almighty to come into manifestation as above, so below. It is the means whereby the kingdom of God becomes a reality here and now through the power of the spoken word. It may be short or long and usually is marked by a formal preamble and a closing, or acceptance.

Deva. Sanskrit for "radiant being." Member of an order of angelic beings who serve with the elemental forces of nature, assisting them to perform their various functions. Angel devas are the guardian spirits of the mountains and the forests. They also ensoul and hold the matrix for the *Christ consciousness* to be outpictured by the people of a particular locale—city, state, nation, or continent—or for a particular race, nationality, or ethnic group.

Dharma. Sanskrit for "law." The realization of the law of selfhood through adherence to cosmic law, including the laws of nature and a spiritual code of conduct such as the way or dharma of the Buddha or the Christ. One's duty to fulfill one's raison d'être through the law of love and the *sacred labor*.

Diamond heart. A concentration of the fires of the will of God which coalesce as a diamond matrix in the hearts of those who are devoted to God's will. Hence, a term used to describe the heart of the *ascended masters,* angel *devas,* and *chelas* devoted to the will of God; often associated with Mary the Mother of Jesus and *El Morya*. The diamond heart of God possesses the quality of the diamond crystal, refracting the *light* of love throughout the creation and reflecting, magnifying, and projecting the virtues embodied by the *sons and daughters of God*.

El Morya Khan, the ascended master. Lord *(Chohan)* of the First *Ray* of God's Will, Chief of the *Darjeeling Council* of the *Great White Brotherhood,* founder of *The Summit Lighthouse,* teacher and sponsor of the *messengers* Mark and Elizabeth Prophet. El Morya was embodied as the Irish poet Thomas Moore, Akbar the Great, Sir Thomas More, Thomas à Becket, and Melchior, one of the three wise men.

Elohim. The seven Spirits of God (Rev. 5:6) who focus the *seven rays* of God's consciousness at cosmic levels. They are the highest among the servants of the LORD known as the builders of form. The hierarchs of the elements governing the planes of earth, air, fire, and water and all elemental beings, *devas,* and forces of nature serve under their direction. In them is personified God as the Creator, the Preserver, and the Destroyer. The Elohim govern the cycles of the outbreath and the inbreath of God throughout the Cosmic Egg. They are the "morning stars" which sang together (Job 38:7) in the creation of the worlds. Their "song" is the music of the spheres, the cosmic chord that holds every galaxy and molecule of *Matter* in its accorded place.

The names of the seven mighty Elohim and their divine complements serving on the seven rays are as follows: first ray, Hercules and Amazonia; second ray, Apollo and Lumina; third ray, Heros and Amora; fourth ray, Purity and Astrea; fifth ray, *Cyclopea* and Virginia; sixth ray, Peace and Aloha; seventh ray, Arcturus and Victoria.

Etheric. Of or relating to that plane of *Matter* which vibrates at the highest frequency capable of being contained in Matter. The etheric frequency and its correspondent plane of consciousness is the repository of the fiery blueprint of the entire physical universe. Etheric energies provide the envelope or vehicle of the soul (etheric or memory body) and the plane of transition between the material and the spiritual universe.

Etheric plane. The highest plane in the dimension of *Matter;* a plane which is as concrete and real (and more so) as the physical plane but which is experienced through the senses of the soul in a dimension and a consciousness beyond physical awareness. The plane on which the records of mankind's entire evolution register individually and collectively.

Etheric temples. Retreats of the *ascended masters* focused in the *etheric plane* or in the plane of the earth; anchoring points for cosmic energies and flames of God; places where the ascended masters train their *chelas* and to which the souls of mankind travel while out of their physical bodies.

Feminine ray. The *light* emanation that comes forth from the Mother aspect of God.

Four lower bodies. *See* Bodies of man.

Gautama Buddha. Born approximately 560 B.C. Prince Siddhartha Gautama of the Sakya clan in Kapilavastu in northern India. Responding to the pulsations of the flame of the Ancient of Days (Lord Sanat Kumara), Prince Siddhartha left family, wife, and son, position, wealth, and power to seek enlightenment. After six years of wandering and experimenting with various yogic disciplines, he attained enlightenment in meditation under the Bo tree near Gaya, India, in which state he remained for a total of forty-nine days. He spent forty-eight years preaching the Eightfold Path, the way of Buddhic enlightenment. Gautama Buddha ascended in approximately 480 B.C.

On January 1, 1956, he assumed the position in *hierarchy* of Lord of the World, enabling Sanat Kumara, his guru and predecessor, to return to his home star, Venus. In his retreat at Shamballa (on the *etheric plane* over the Gobi Desert), Gautama Buddha "keeps" the *threefold flame* of life on behalf of the evolutions of the planet. Each year at the Wesak Festival (the full moon in May) he addresses his disciples on several planes from a valley of the Himalayas. In his annual New Year's Eve address given at the Royal Teton Retreat, he releases the thought form for the year to members of the hierarchy and certain unascended *chelas*.

Goal-fitting. A term used by *El Morya* to describe the fitting of the evolving soul consciousness for the goal of reunion with God; a process of discipline and initiation which souls preparing for the *ascension* undergo under the direction of the *ascended masters*.

God and Goddess Meru. *See* Meru, God and Goddess.

Goddess of Liberty. The ascended lady master who holds the *cosmic consciousness* of liberty for the earth. While embodied on *Atlantis,* she erected the Temple of the Sun where Manhattan Island now is. With the sinking of Atlantis the physical temple was destroyed, but the etheric counterpart remains on the *etheric plane* where she continues to focus the flame of liberty on the central altar surrounded by twelve shrines dedicated to the twelve hierarchies of the sun. The Goddess of Liberty is the spokesman for the *Karmic Board* and represents the second *ray* on the board.

Goddess of Purity. The ascended lady master whose awareness of the purity of God has reached the level of *cosmic consciousness* and who has thereby earned the title in *hierarchy* of Goddess of Purity. She serves to focus God's awareness of himself as the flame of purity—the pure white *light*.

Godfré Ray King. *See* Ballard, Guy W.

God Self. *See* I AM Presence.

Golden age. A cycle of enlightenment, peace, and harmony wherein the souls of mankind merge in the Christ flame for the fulfillment of the divine plan "as above, so below" through "thy kingdom on earth as it is in heaven."

Great Central Sun. The nucleus or white-fire core of the Cosmic Egg. (The God Star Sirius is the focus of the Great Central Sun in our sector of the galaxy.)

Great Divine Director. An *ascended master* whose attainment of *cosmic consciousness* enables him to ensoul the flame of divine direction throughout the universe. Founder of the

House of Rakoczy, teacher of *Saint Germain,* sponsor and Manu of the *seventh root race,* and representing the first *ray* on the *Karmic Board.*

Great White Brotherhood. The fraternity of saints, sages, and *ascended masters* of all ages who, coming from every nation, race and religion, have reunited with the *Spirit* of the living God and who comprise the heavenly hosts. The term "white" refers to the halo of white *light* that surrounds their forms. The Great White Brotherhood also includes in its ranks certain unascended *chelas* of the ascended masters.

Guru. Sanskrit for "spiritual leader" or "teacher." The highest gurus are the *ascended masters*—mankind's teachers who will be fully recognized in the Aquarian Age.

Hierarchy. The chain of individualized beings fulfilling aspects of God's infinite selfhood. Hierarchy is the means whereby God in the *Great Central Sun* steps down the energies of his consciousness, that succeeding evolutions in time and space might come to know the wonder of his love.

Hilarion. *See* Chohan.

I AM Presence. The I AM THAT I AM; the individualized Presence of God focused for each individual soul. The God-identity of the individual; the Divine Monad; the individual Source. The origin of the soul focused in the planes of *Spirit* just above the physical form; the personification of the God flame for the individual.

Ich dien. German for "I serve." Motto of Clara Louise Kieninger's class at Lutheran Hospital School of Nursing in St. Louis; motto of the Prince of Wales.

Karma. Sanskrit for action or deed. Karma is (1) energy in action; (2) the law of cause and effect and retribution. "Whatsoever a man soweth, that shall he also reap." (Gal. 6:7) Thus the law of karma decrees that from lifetime to lifetime man determines his fate by his actions—thoughts, feelings, words, and deeds.

Karma yoga. The path of reunion with God fulfilled through the balancing of *karma,* through service to life, through working the works of God on earth, through action.

Karmic Board. *See* Lords of Karma.

Keepers of the Flame Fraternity. Founded in 1961 by *Saint Germain,* an organization of *chelas* of the *ascended masters* who support the activities of the *Great White Brotherhood* and the dissemination of their teachings on earth and who receive graded lessons in cosmic law dictated by the ascended masters through their *messengers* Mark and Elizabeth Prophet.

Keynote. That aspect of the music of the spheres which fulfills the electronic blueprint of the soul in the sound *ray.* A specific melody that registers as the harmony and frequency of the soul. The keynote of the *ascended masters* can be heard with the inner ear when they are at hand.

Kuthumi, the ascended master. The Master K.H., cofounder (with *El Morya,* known as the Master M.) of the Theosophical movement in 1875 through Helena Petrovna Blavatsky. Head of the order of the Brothers of the Golden Robe; serving with Jesus in the office of World Teacher; formerly *Chohan* of the Second *Ray.* Kuthumi was embodied as Shah Jahan, Saint Francis of Assisi, Balthazar, one of the three wise men, and Pythagoras.

Light. Spiritual light is the energy of God, the potential of the Christ. As the essence of *Spirit,* the term "light" can be used synonymously with the terms "God,", "Christ," and *"sacred fire."* It is the emanation of the *Great Central Sun* and the individualized *I AM Presence.*

Lords of Karma. The beings who make up the Karmic Board: *the Goddess of Liberty;* the *Great Divine Director;* Portia, the Goddess of Justice; the ascended lady master Nada; Pallas Athena, Goddess of Truth; Kuan Yin, Goddess of Mercy; the Elohim *Cyclopea;* and the Dhyani Buddha Vairochana. These eight *ascended masters* dispense justice to this system of worlds. All souls must pass before the Karmic Board before and after each incarnation on earth. The Karmic Board, acting in consonance with the individual *I AM Presence* and *Christ Self,* determines when the soul has earned the right to be free from the wheel of *karma* and the round of rebirth.

Lotus. *See* Ballard, Edna.

Lucifer. From the Latin, meaning "light-bearer." One who attained the rank of *archangel* and fell from grace through ambition, the pride of the ego, and disobedience to the laws of God. The *angels* who followed him are the fallen ones, also called Luciferians or sons of Belial, who have embodied among the children of God. (See the parable of the tares among the wheat, Matt. 13:24–30, 36–43.)

Luciferians. The *angels* who followed *Lucifer* in his rebellion against God.

Maha Chohan. The representative of the Holy Spirit to a planet and its evolutions. The *ascended master* who currently holds the office of Great Lord (Maha Chohan) over the seven lords (chohans) of the rays was embodied as the poet Homer. In his final embodiment in India, the *light* which he drew forth was a comfort to millions. The Maha Chohan maintains an *etheric* retreat with a physical focus on the island of Ceylon where the flame of the Holy Spirit is anchored. *See also* Chohan.

Manu. Sanskrit for the progenitor and lawgiver of the human race. *Twin Flames* assigned by the Father-Mother God to ensoul the archetypal pattern of the Christ for certain evolutions or lifewaves which comprise what is known as a *root race.*

Mater. Latin for "mother." Mater is the *mater*ialization of the God flame, the feminine polarity of the Godhead. The term is used interchangeably with "Matter" to describe the planes of being that conform with the aspect of God as Mother. The soul that descends from the plane of *Spirit* abides in time and space in Mater for the purpose of its evolution that necessitates the mastery of time and space and of the energies of God through the correct exercise of free will. The four lower *bodies of man,* of a planet, and of systems of worlds occupy and make up the frequencies of Matter. *See also* Spirit.

Matter. *See* Mater.

Meru, God and Goddess. The *ascended masters* who hold the focus of the *feminine ray* for the planet in the *etheric* retreat over Lake Titicaca on the Peru-Bolivia boundary. The God and Goddess Meru are the *Manus* of the sixth *root race*. Lord and Lady Meru were given the title "God" and "Goddess" because of their *cosmic consciousness* of the Mother ray (Me-ru).

Messenger. One appointed by the *hierarchy* to deliver to mankind the dictations of the *ascended masters* ex cathedra in the power of the spoken word. One who is trained by an ascended master to receive by various methods the words, concepts, teachings, and messages of the *Great White Brotherhood*. One who delivers the law, the prophecies, and the dispensations of God for a people and an age.

Mother flame. That pulsation of the *sacred fire* which focuses the Mother or feminine aspect of God.

Motherhouse. From 1970 to 1983, West Coast center of the *Keepers of the Flame Fraternity* in Santa Barbara, California, dedicated to the Divine Mother. Here the *ascended masters'* university was founded by Mark and Elizabeth Prophet in July 1971.

Mother Mary. The mother of Jesus, who ascended at the close of her Galilean embodiment. Her name means mother ray *(Ma ray)*. She was embodied on *Atlantis* as a temple virgin and tended the flame in the Temple of Truth while learning the science of the immaculate concept which enabled her to give birth to the Christ in her final incarnation.

Mother of the Flame. An office of *hierarchy* held successively by those unascended feminine devotees appointed by the *Great White Brotherhood* to nourish, or mother, the flame of life in all mankind. In 1961 Clara Louise Kieninger was named the first Mother of the Flame of the *Keepers of the Flame Fraternity* by *Saint Germain*. On April 9, 1966, that office was transferred to Elizabeth Clare Prophet. At that time Clara Louise Kieninger became the Regent Mother of the Flame, an office which she continues to hold from the ascended level.

Omega. Divine counterpart of Alpha. Alpha and Omega are *twin flames* who hold the awareness of God in the *Great Central Sun* in the white fire core of our *cosmos*. They are mentioned in the Book of Revelation as the beginning and the ending (Rev. 1:8). Thus the Father is the origin and the Mother is the fulfillment of the cycles of God's consciousness throughout the creation.

Pearls of Wisdom. Weekly letters of instruction dictated by the *ascended masters* to their *chelas* throughout the world through the *messengers* Mark and Elizabeth Prophet. The *Pearls of Wisdom* have been published by *The Summit Lighthouse* since 1958.

Rays. Beams of *light* or radiant energy. The light emanations of the Godhead which, when invoked in the name of God or in the name of the Christ, burst forth as a flame in the world of the individual. Rays may be projected through the God consciousness of ascended or unascended beings as a concentration of energy taking on numerous God-qualities, such as love, truth, wisdom, healing, etc. Through the misuse of God's energy, certain unascended beings may project rays having negative qualities, such as death rays, sleep rays, hypnotic rays, disease rays, etc. *See also* Color rays.

Real Image. (1) The true image of God after which man (male and female) was made in the beginning (Gen. 1:26–27). The Real Image is the likeness of God; it is the blueprint of the true identity of the *sons and daughters of God*. (2) The face of God.

Real Self. The *Christ Self;* the I AM Presence; immortal *Spirit* that is the animating principle of all *man*ifestation.

Reembodiment. Alternate term for reincarnation—the action of reincarnating; the state of being reincarnated. Rebirth in new bodies or forms of life, especially a rebirth of a soul in a new human body. The term "reembodiment" is preferred by the *ascended masters,* whose teaching distinguishes the law of karma and reembodiment from the Hindu doctrine of reincarnation, or the transmigration of souls. The latter assumes that souls may reincarnate in either a human or an animal form, whereas the ascended masters teach that the human soul can reembody only in a human form. They teach that the soul continues to return to the physical plane in a new body temple until it has balanced its *karma,* attained self-mastery, overcome the cycles of time and space, and finally attained reunion with the *I AM Presence* through the ritual of the *ascension.*

Retreat of the Resurrection Spiral. Physical retreat of the *Great White Brotherhood* dedicated by *Omega* on April 11, 1971. Until 1976, international headquarters of *The Summit Lighthouse* in Colorado Springs, Colorado, where the resurrection flame was anchored on the *etheric plane.* In 1985, at the time of the passing of the property into other hands, the *light* of the entire retreat and forcefield was withdrawn and held in the *etheric* octave until the opening of the vast Retreat of the Divine Mother over the Royal Teton Ranch and adjacent park and wilderness lands.

Root Race. A group of souls, or a lifewave, who embody as a group and have a unique archetypal pattern, divine plan, and mission to fulfill on earth. According to esoteric tradition, there are seven primary aggregations of souls, i.e., the first to the *seventh root races.*

Sacred Fire. God, *light,* life, energy, the I AM THAT I AM. "Our God is a consuming fire." (Heb. 12:29) The sacred fire is the precipitation of the Holy Ghost for the baptism of souls, for purification, for alchemy and transmutation, and for the realization of the sacred ritual of the return to the One.

Sacred labor. That particular calling, livelihood, or profession whereby one establishes his soul's worth both to himself and to his fellowman. One perfects his sacred labor developing his God-given talents as well as the gifts and graces of the Holy Spirit and laying these upon the altar of service to humanity. The sacred labor is not only one's contribution to one's community, but it is the means whereby the soul can balance the *threefold flame* and pass the tests of the *seven rays*. It is an indispensable component of the path to reunion with God through the giving of oneself in practical living for God.

Saint Germain, the ascended master. Lord *(Chohan)* of the Seventh *Ray*. Hierarch of the Aquarian Age, patron of the United States of America. Saint Germain was accorded the title "God of Freedom" because of his intense devotion to the flame of freedom and his attainment of the *cosmic consciousness* of that flame. He was embodied as Francis Bacon; Christopher Columbus; Merlin; Joseph, the protector of Jesus and Mary; and the prophet Samuel.

Serapis Bey, the ascended master. Lord *(Chohan)* of the Fourth *Ray;* Hierarch of the Ascension Temple at Luxor, Egypt; keeper of the *ascension* flame. Known as the great disciplinarian, Serapis reviews and trains candidates for the ascension.

Seven rays. *See* Color rays.

Seventh root race. An evolution of souls destined to embody on the continent of South America under the seventh dispensation, the Aquarian Age, and the seventh *ray. See also* Root race.

Sons and daughters of God. Those who come forth as the fruit of the divine union of the spirals of Alpha and *Omega;* those who have the potential to become the Christ. The creation of the Father-Mother God, made in the image and likeness of the Divine Us, identified by the *threefold flame* of life anchored within the heart. The term "sons and daughters of God" denotes a level of initiation and a rank in *hierarchy* that is above those who are called the children of God—

Glossary 225

children in the sense that they have not passed the initiations of the *sacred fire* that would warrant their being called sons and daughters of God.

Spirit. (1) The masculine polarity of the Godhead; the coordinate of Matter; God as Father, who of necessity includes within the polarity of himself God as Mother and hence is known as the Father-Mother God. The plane of the *I AM Presence,* of perfection; the dwelling place of the *ascended masters* in the Most High God. (When lower-cased, as in "spirits," the term is synonymous with discarnates, or disembodied souls.) (2) The Holy Spirit. *See also* Mater.

Summit Beacon. Newsletter of *The Summit Lighthouse* published by the *Keepers of the Flame Fraternity* from 1965 to 1978.

The Summit Lighthouse. An outer organization of the *Great White Brotherhood* founded by Mark L. Prophet in 1958 in Washington D.C., under the direction of the ascended master *El Morya,* Chief of the *Darjeeling Council,* for the purpose of publishing and disseminating the teachings of the *ascended masters.*

Summit University. The university of the *Great White Brotherhood* sponsored by the *ascended masters* and founded in 1971 by Mark and Elizabeth Prophet in Santa Barbara, California. The program of 12-week seminars was inaugurated in September 1973 by Elizabeth with the dispensation from Gautama Buddha—"a torch charged with the vital fires from God's heavenly altar and the conveyance of a vast mission to illumine the world's children and produce the blessing of true culture to the age and unto all people everywhere." The university offers a comprehensive curriculum in cosmic law and the teachings of the ascended masters.

Synthetic Image. That aspect of man or woman which is the counterfeit of true selfhood. The synthetic image is diametrically opposed to the *Real Image* of the *Christ Self*, which is the true identity of the *sons and daughters of God*.

Temple of the Resurrection. Retreat of the Holy City located on the *etheric plane* over Jerusalem. The retreat is under the direction of Jesus and Mary. The resurrection flame is anchored there.

Threefold flame. The flame of the Christ that is the spark of life anchored in the heart chakra, or heart center, of the *sons and daughters of God* and the children of God. The sacred trinity of power, wisdom, and love that is the manifestation of the *sacred fire*.

Transfiguration. An initiation on the path of the *ascension* which takes place when the initiate has attained a certain balance and expansion of the *threefold flame*. (See Matt. 17:1–8.)

Transition. (1) Transition of the soul and the consciousness from one plane of being to another. (2) The change called death; the change from the abode of the soul in the physical body to another body. As Paul said, "There are also celestial bodies and bodies terrestrial." (I Cor. 15:40)

Twin Flame. The soul's masculine or feminine counterpart conceived out of the same white-fire core, the fiery ovoid of the *I AM Presence*.

Violet Flame. Seventh-*ray* aspect of the Holy Spirit. The *sacred fire* that transmutes the cause, effect, record and memory of sin, or negative *karma*. Also called the flame of transmutation, of freedom, and of forgiveness. (See *The Science of the Spoken Word* by Mark and Elizabeth Prophet, published by Summit University Press.)

FOR MORE INFORMATION

Summit University Press books are available at fine bookstores worldwide and at your favorite online bookseller. For a free catalog of our books and products or to learn more about the spiritual techniques featured in this book, please contact:

Summit University Press
PO Box 5000
Corwin Springs, MT 59030-5000 USA
Telephone: 1-800-245-5445 or 406-848-9500
Fax: 1-800-221-8307 or 406-848-9555
www.summituniversitypress.com
info@summituniversitypress.com

Printed by Libri Plureos GmbH in Hamburg, Germany